LIFE TOUCHED WITH WONDER

LIFE TOUCHED WITH WONDER

DOORWAYS of FAITH

FROM THE EDITORS OF READER'S DIGEST

THE READER'S DIGEST ASSOCIATION, INC.
PLEASANTVILLE, NEW YORK

Copyright © 2001 The Reader's Digest Association, Inc.

All rights reserved. Unauthorized reproduction, in any manner, is prohibited.

ISBN 0-7621-8869-3

Printed in the United States of America

Book design by Patrice Sheridan

Reader's Digest and the Pegasus logo are registered trademarks of The Reader's Digest Association, Inc.

You can also visit us on the World Wide Web at http://www.rd.com

CONTENTS

INTRODUCTION

Men wonder at the height of mountains, the huge waves of the sea, the broad flow of rivers, the course of the stars—and forget to wonder at themselves.
                                                            —*Saint Augustine*

We feel awe when we see a grand landscape or view the majesty of a starry sky. But there's also wonder in a child's kiss when you're feeling down, in a friend's unexpected recovery from a frightening illness, in a walk on a hushed, snowy night. Such moments take us by surprise and lift us from the mundane and the familiar. Suddenly, inexplicably, we catch a glimpse of a reality beyond ourselves, and see evidence that there is something beautiful, merciful, loving knit into the fabric of creation—even in ourselves.

In fact, ordinary people can be the most gifted messengers of wonder. Their stories offer compelling evidence of the power of the spirit in daily life. In this new book series we have selected the best of such true-life stories and present them in separate volumes organized around themes.

In *Doorways of Faith,* you will find stories of people from all walks of life whose unshakable belief in God's power strengthened them in unforeseen ways. Their examples may even inspire you to find—and trust—God's guiding hand in your own life.

MY ANGEL
IN DISGUISE

BY
JAMES DODSON

*S*everal winters ago, around Christmastime, I ran over a boy on a sled. He flew out of nowhere during a serious snowstorm, a small figure darting down a steep farmyard into the road just as my Blazer came over a knoll. Through the veil of snow, I caught only the briefest glimpse of him—an impression of startled eyes behind eyeglasses, a blue parka—before I sharply cut the wheel.

I remember hearing the awful crunch, a muffled cry, and then my truck was sliding down a steep incline, plowing sideways through deep drifts, coming to rest almost on its side. I sat there with groceries strewn all over the place for perhaps ten seconds. Then I ripped off my shoulder belt, kicked open the door with my boot, and clawed my way through the knee-deep snow back up the bank. The boy was lying in the middle of the road, eerily still. "My legs. My legs," he cried softly. "I can't move my legs."

Crouching by his side, I remember thinking two things with an almost military clarity. First, I had to get him out of the road or we would both be run over by the next vehicle to come over the knoll.

Second, this kid was going to die or at least never walk again because I'd crushed him.

As I knelt there with snow pouring down like cinders from heaven, a flood of soft paternal words began flowing from my mouth. "Listen to me, son. You're going to be okay. But first we have to get you off the road. Try and relax. Everything will be fine."

I don't know whom I was trying to convince most. He closed his eyes, nodded, and I moved his limp body gently to the shoulder, aware that I could be doing even more damage—severing what was left of a mangled spinal cord or destroying whatever muscle tissue or nerve connections remained. But I couldn't risk a plow truck roaring down on us at any second.

"Can you move your fingers?" I said.

"Yes," he replied, and showed me. Snowflakes were accumulating and melting on his flushed face. I studied his eyes to see if he was slipping into shock. They were clear. I guessed that he was 12 or 13 years old—a good-looking kid, I realized, and damn brave.

Then from behind us rose a heartrending wail. I turned and saw a large, coatless woman struggling to maneuver through the snow, two children in her wake. "Oh, my God, oh, my God!" she cried. She lost her footing and tumbled comically into the drift at the bottom of the driveway, and I had no option but to go help her out. I extended her my hand and pulled her from the drift. Her face was a mask of anguish, the face of a mother confronted with the unthinkable.

We stood there in each other's odd embrace for a moment, performing a little minuet on the slippery road, staring briefly into each other's eyes until we heard a small sound, and we simultaneously turned to face the boy.

He was standing up.

"It's okay, Mom," he said, rubbing his back. "I think I'm okay."

His name was Matthew, and he was the son of a church caretaker. He sat on a chair in his mother's warm kitchen, holding back sobs.

"Why are you crying, Matthew?" asked his mother. "Are you injured?"

"No," he said with a trembling voice. "I was just thinking . . . I don't know why I wasn't killed."

His younger sister Rose explained what had happened. When school was called off for the day, they'd gone into the back meadow to sled. But the farm's steeper front yard tempted them. They never even considered the danger of the road.

"I could've been killed," Matthew repeated, in a kind of daze. "I don't know why I wasn't killed."

"Because we were both incredibly lucky," I answered.

"I think it was a miracle," said his mother.

Later, I went outside to watch the wrecker winch my truck out. Both tires were flattened; the fender was bent. "I don't see how you missed running clean over him. It's amazing," said the police officer, indicating the intersecting skid pattern and sled track.

"Damn near a miracle," piped up the driver of the wrecker.

I went back to say good-bye to Matthew and his mother. He'd gone to lie down, and his mother thanked me profusely. We actually embraced, and she began to cry. I told her I would call in a day or so to see how everyone was doing.

"Are you okay?" she asked, studying me.

"Yes," I replied. "I'm fine."

But I wasn't. In fact, I had never been more deeply shaken in my life. No matter what the police officer had said, I knew that the boy had disappeared under the front of my truck, yet somehow survived with only an angry red welt on the small of his back to show for it. I just couldn't explain it.

I, too, might have said it was a miracle, if I believed in such things. But miracles have always struck me as the cheap parlor tricks of faith—things cited by Vegas-style preachers to keep the crowd interested and the tithes flowing.

I went home and sat for a couple of hours watching chickadees dive-bomb our bird feeder. I didn't feel like moving or talking. My wife took our two small children, Maggie and Jack, out shopping. As I sat there, alone, the movie projector between my ears played the accident over and over.

Before I hit Matthew, I had been having what my wife calls my "annual Christmas crisis," a private little tempest of the soul that begins somewhere around the winter solstice, when darkness descends like a closing curtain and news programs flood us with the year's most memorable human and natural disasters.

On the morning of the big snowstorm I was still in a funk, and I couldn't understand why. And so, at the height of the storm, disgusted with my disgust, I decided to go to the grocery store. It was empty save for a lone clerk totaling the items of an elderly woman. She was buying a magazine and a potted plant. I noticed she was wearing running shoes instead of boots. "It's beautiful outside, isn't it?" she said, smiling at me. "But you know, some people always drive too fast when it's snowing."

Kooky old bird, I said to myself. But I smiled back and agreed. Then I got back in my Blazer and headed home. Turning onto Meadow Cross Road, however, I kept thinking about what she had said. As I approached the knoll by the farm, I cut my speed by half. An instant later, Matthew flew under my wheels.

In the aftermath of the accident I kept wondering how to say thank-you to someone who enters your life for 15 seconds? All I knew about her was that she likes houseplants and could use a new pair of boots. Then I happened across a copy of *Time* magazine, with, of all things, a painting of an angel on its cover. "The New Age of Angels" read the headline.

I started reading. "In her best-selling collection of angel encounters, *A Book of Angels,*" the article said, "author Sophy Burnham writes that angels disguise themselves—as a dream, a comforting presence, a pulse of energy, a person—to ensure that the message is received, even if the messenger is explained away. 'It is not that skeptics do not experience the mysterious and divine,' she explains, 'but rather that the mysteries are presented to them in such an everyday, reasonable way so as not to disturb.' "

Once again, I sat in my den mulling this one over. I considered the possibility that my guardian angel was an old lady in sneakers who thought the world would be a better place if we all slowed down and noticed the passing scenery.

Our church's Christmas Eve service that winter was held in a freezing barn, with real sheep and a bracing air of fresh manure—just the kind of place you'd expect the Son of Man to pick for a nursery suite. An overflow crowd—mostly families with small kids—heard St. Matthew's account of the virgin birth, and then, as we went back out into the night, the snow began to fall again as if on cue.

When we got home, four-year-old Maggie took my hand, then suddenly let go and ran and flopped in the yard. Her younger brother, Jack, followed on her heels, falling with his arms joyously outspread.

"Look, Daddy," Maggie cried out. "Snow angels!"

Frankly, I'd completely forgotten about snow angels. But I think the ones my children made that Christmas Eve were outstanding.

Even more amazing, in the morning they were still there.

An angel collects all the prayers offered in
the synagogues, weaves them into garlands,
and puts them on God's head.

MEIR

CHILD CHOKING!

BY

LES BROWN, WITH ANNAMAE CHENEY

*D*readed words: "Child choking! Handle Code Three!" I responded immediately, flipping on red lights and siren as the dispatcher gave directions. *Just my luck,* I thought as I sped off.

I had barely begun my working day as a deputy sheriff in San Diego, California. Actually it was my day off, and I had been called in to cover for an officer who was ill. I knew next to nothing about this particular beat and had intended to drive around to familiarize myself with the area. Now my first call was a life-and-death emergency several miles away.

I decided to take the unfinished freeway; it was next to impossible to get through the traffic on Highway 101. Just ahead was the street that would take me to my destination. Then, anguish swept through me. There was no "off" ramp! Between me and that road was a deep, wide ditch and a steep embankment.

Tires screeched as I stopped, red lights still flashing. I got out and looked at the busy road so far below.

God help me! I cried out silently. *There's no time to get another car here. What am I going to do?*

"What's the matter, officer?"

I looked up, and saw a man sitting on top of a gigantic earthmoving vehicle. He must have been two stories high.

"Child choking to death! I have to get down there, but there's no road. If I go around, I'll never make it."

Years of discipline had taught me to control my emotions, but I was in an agony of frustration.

"Follow me, officer—I'll *make* you a road!"

I took off after him, amazed at what his mammoth machine could do. The huge scoops on either end of it were full of dirt. He dumped them into the ditch.

Hurry! Hurry! Hurry! The clock had become my enemy.

The earthmover started down the long sloping embankment, scattering dirt. Clouds of dust enveloped us. It seemed like hours, but in reality it was a short time until the earthmover lumbered down onto the highway, blocking traffic.

I raced, siren screaming, the few short blocks to the address I had been given. As I burst through the doorway, a terrified mother handed me her baby. He was already blue. *Was I too late? God help me!*

All I remember about the next few seconds was grabbing the baby and automatically carrying out the emergency procedures I'd been trained to perform. An object flew from his throat onto the floor. It was a button that had mercifully let a tiny bit of air through.

A fireman rushed into the room.

Precious oxygen.

The child screamed, turned red, flailed his tiny fists. He was angry, but he was very much alive.

Back in my car, I logged the incident, reported in by radio, and drove away, shaken but elated.

I glanced upward. *Thank you* was my unspoken thought.

9

Lately I had found myself wondering if life in law enforcement was really worthwhile—the hostile, the criminals, the dregs of society; the petty things that took time and energy to deal with. This was a thankless job. Was it what I wanted?

Yet, with God's help, I had just saved a life. And, in this act, my own life had come into perspective. That little one in distress had taught me I had important work to do.

As I drove along the next day, I approached the place where I had stood in desperation 24 hours before. I slowed as I saw the earthmover. I wanted to thank the driver.

He ran toward me and stammered, "The . . . the baby . . ." He stopped, too deeply moved to speak.

Surprised at his emotion, I tried to reassure him. "The baby is all right. Thanks to you—you helped save his life. Man, that was teamwork."

He gulped, "I . . . I know. But what I didn't know then was . . ." He bit his lip hard, and added in a whisper, *That was my son.*

Faith is a sounder guide than reason.

Reason can go only so far, but faith has no

limits.

BLAISE PASCAL

STEFANIA'S CHOICE

BY

THOMAS FLEMING

Stefania Podgorska had just put her young sister Helena to bed when a knock rattled the front door, sending a chill through the 19-year-old. For over three years, southeastern Poland had been part of Hitler's empire. It was 1942, and Przemysl, a city of more than 50,000, was full of grim-eyed Gestapo agents and soldiers on their way to the Russian front.

Blond, beautiful Stefania had felt their eyes on her more than once as she entered the house where she lived alone with eight-year-old Helena. Their father had died before the war, and their mother and brother had been deported to Germany as forced laborers. To support herself and her sister, Stefania worked as a machine-tool operator at a local factory.

Was this visitor, she wondered, a soldier offering to "protect" her? Heart pounding, Stefania opened the door a crack. There stood a battered, stocky man in muddy clothes. He slumped against the doorjamb and whispered, "Fusia, I need help."

Fusia. It was a nickname used only by close friends. Stefania recognized the grisly figure as Josef Burzminski, 27, a son of the couple in whose household Stefania had worked when the Germans occupied Przemysl. A few months before, the Nazis had herded his family into the ghetto, along with the rest of the city's 20,000 Jews. Before the parents left, they asked Stefania, whom they considered a trusted family friend, to stay in their house to protect it.

Stefania helped Josef to a chair. "Can I stay with you one night, Fusia?" he asked. "I swear I'll go tomorrow. I don't want to endanger you."

Stefania struggled to control the raw fear that gripped her. German notices posted throughout Przemysl warned that anyone who hid Jews would be executed. She wanted to help this desperate man, but could she risk not only her own life but Helena's as well?

From all the teachings of her parents, especially her mother, Stefania knew what she should do. Along with a strong religious faith, Katarzyna Podgorska had instilled in her daughter a powerful sense of right and wrong. Stefania recalled a day in her childhood when her mother had seen some children abusing a young boy because he was Jewish. Katarzyna had rebuked them, telling Stefania that she hoped she would never do such a thing. "We're all children of the same God," her mother said.

Now, looking beyond the doorway to the bedroom, Stefania glimpsed a painting of the Blessed Virgin. She had found the picture at a fair when she was nine and had begged her mother to buy it. Each night when Stefania prayed, the serene face soothed and strengthened her.

You must do it, a voice now whispered in Stefania's heart. She placed her hand on Josef's bruised cheek. "Of course you may stay," she told him.

While she made tea, Josef explained what had happened. The Nazi SS had swept through the ghetto, loading Josef's parents and many others into boxcars destined for the death camps. Josef and one of his brothers were later forced aboard another train. As it hauled them away, Josef used a pocketknife to cut the barbed wire on a small window high up the boxcar wall. Squeezing his short, muscular body through the opening, he thudded to the ground with terrific force.

When he regained consciousness, he stumbled along the tracks toward Przemysl, hiding in the woods. "This was the only place I thought to go," Josef said as he gratefully devoured the bread Stefania put before him.

After two weeks, Josef felt strong enough to leave. Sneaking back into the ghetto, he found his youngest brother, Henek, and Henek's wife, Danuta, near starvation. Old family friend Doctor William Shylenger and his daughter Judy, along with their friend, a widowed dentist in his late 50s, and his 20-year-old son, were also in a desperate state.

Josef bribed a printer for a fake identity card that allowed him to move about the city, smuggling food to the others with Stefania's help. But after he lost the card and had to knock out an SS trooper who stopped him, this tough, daring Jew realized the game could not go on. He made his way back to Stefania's.

"Fusia, would you hide some of us? Without your help, we can't survive."

For a moment Stefania had wondered if Josef had gone crazy. The war could last ten years. "A lot of people can't hide under my bed every time someone knocks on my door," she said.

Stefania knew that both she and her sister might die if they sheltered this man. But she would be dead in spirit if she abandoned him. "If I can find such a house, I'll do it," she finally said.

But where? Eventually she discovered 3 Tatarska Street, a semi-detached cottage with two rooms, a kitchen and an attic. After checking with Josef, she rented it and started cleaning up and hanging dark curtains so no one could see in.

Soon the fugitives began arriving. First came Josef and the dentist's son. Then Doctor Shylenger and his daughter, followed by the dentist, a grave, bearded man who wept with relief when he reached safety.

No sooner had they settled in than a note arrived from a friend of the dentist's, a widow still in the ghetto. She wanted to join them with her son and daughter—hinting that if she were turned down, she might report them. Angrily, Stefania agreed to accept her.

The dentist then begged Stefania to admit his nephew and his wife, who were hiding in an abandoned building. Next, Henek and Danuta joined the group.

Last to come was a Jewish mailman who had heard of the house on Tatarska Street. Once more Stefania agreed, swelling the number of fugitives to 13. That she had made the right decision would become brutally clear when the Przemysl ghetto's remaining Jews were herded off to the death camps.

Using boards Stefania bought, Josef built a false wall in the attic. There was just enough room behind its cleverly disguised door for all 13 to sleep.

Scarcely had he finished when Stefania came home with unnerving news. "An SS man lives next door!"

Now the group was even more fearful of making too much noise. Because several fugitives snored, Josef appointed night monitors, and the snorers were prodded into silence.

Visits by Stefania's friends were also a problem. Usually she managed to ease them out quickly. But one young man, proclaiming his love for her, began visiting almost nightly. During one visit the dentist almost suffocated himself in the attic, trying to muffle a coughing fit.

"That's enough!" said Josef after the ardent suitor left. He told Stefania to buy a picture of the handsomest German officer she could find and hang it on her wall. That night, when her suitor arrived, he asked, "Who's that?"

"My new boyfriend," Stefania said. Out went the suitor, never to be seen again at 3 Tatarska Street.

Without risk,
faith is an impossibility.

SØREN KIERKEGAARD

"We have a case of typhus," the dentist announced one cold winter morning. The widow had come down with it. They tried to isolate her to avoid infecting others. Her fever soared.

One night, the frenzied woman rushed screaming into the moonlit street. Stefania finally got her back into the house. If an informer saw all this, the young woman realized in panic, they were doomed.

Stefania stumbled into the other bedroom and knelt before her painting of Mary. *Save us, not for my sake, but for Helena's,* she prayed.

She turned to find Josef in the doorway. "Did you get an answer?" he asked.

"Yes," Stefania said with calm certainty. "We'll be all right. The Germans won't come."

A few weeks later, another disaster loomed—the fugitives began running out of cash to buy food. "We'll raise money with our hands," Stefania said.

The next day during her factory lunch break, she began knitting a sweater, using yarn from an old one she had unraveled at home. A coworker, admiring it, asked if she would knit one for her, for cash. "Sure," Stefania said.

Soon she had orders for a dozen sweaters. At 3 Tatarska Street, the group worked night and day. Grateful customers never noticed the extraordinary amount of knitting Stefania turned out.

As 1943 waned, Stefania picked up rumors that the Germans were losing the war and retreating. But Josef warned against being too hopeful. "The Germans are still here," he said. "Their mood may grow more vicious as defeat looms."

One day, as Stefania left for work, a police siren wailed. A few blocks away, SS troops surrounded a house, dragged out some terrified Jews and the Polish family who had been hiding them, and flung them against the wall. "Fire!" the SS commander ordered, and machine-gun fire riddled the victims.

Stefania stared dazedly at the bleeding bodies. For the next several weeks, she was unable to sleep. One night, trudging home from work, she wondered how much longer she could endure the ordeal.

As she came in the door, Josef and some of the others were playing hide-and-seek with Helena. The child's eyes sparkled as she raced by, calling, "I'm going to catch you this time, Joe!"

These people are my family, Stefania realized. *I cannot abandon them.*

A few months later, as spring sent warm winds and soft rain swirling through Przemysl, the lookout at the window warned, "SS approaching!" The fugitives scrambled to the attic.

Stefania answered the door. An officer curtly informed her that she had two hours to move out. "Why? What have I done?" she asked.

"The army is setting up a hospital across the street. We need this house for nurses' quarters."

After he left, Stefania rushed to consult Josef. "You and Helena must leave immediately," he said. "Hide in the countryside."

"What are you going to do?"

"Die fighting," Josef answered.

"Before we do anything, I'm going to pray for help," Stefania said.

"Let's all pray," Josef agreed. Ever since he had jumped from the train, a sense of God's protecting hand had been growing within him.

Everyone followed Stefania into her bedroom and knelt.

Stefania concentrated. Long ago, in a shrine at Czestochowa, her Virgin had promised to protect Poland from its enemies. Stefania now asked that her Jewish family be included in this historic vow.

A gentle voice seemed to tell her, *Don't leave—you have nothing to fear. Send your 13 upstairs. Open the windows. Begin cleaning as if you expect to stay. Sing as you work.*

Calmly, Stefania told Josef to take everyone to the attic. "I'm not leaving you," she said. "Everything will be all right." Then she and Helena opened the windows and began spring-cleaning.

Soon the SS officer reappeared. "You won't have to leave after all," he said. "We'll only need one bedroom for two of our nurses."

They were saved—or were they? How could they survive with two Germans in the house? "I'll make sure no one even budges when they're around," Josef assured Stefania. He promised unwavering vigilance.

A week later the nurses moved in. They spent many hours a day at the hospital, but at night they would often bring home German soldiers and retreat to their bedroom for a noisy party.

Fear and tension gripped the fugitives. One afternoon, both nurses came home early with two soldiers carrying rifles. The four talked in low tones. Suddenly one nurse climbed the ladder leading to the attic.

Josef, behind the false wall, heard footsteps and signaled everyone to freeze. Through a pinhole, he saw a blond head appear at the top of the stairs. The nurse looked around, frowning. Moments later, the four Germans left the house. The hideaway had survived its ultimate test.

Then at work the next day, new trouble arose. The German manager announced that the factory was going to be dismantled and moved back to Germany. Stefania's salary vanished.

Now everyone redoubled the knitting efforts. One sweater earned them only enough to eat for three days, and the market for their wares was not dependable. Whole days went by without food. In desperation they chewed pork rind and other scraps Stefania bought on the black market.

One day the nurses rushed back from the hospital in wild agitation. "We're going home to Germany. Come with us—our ward needs a maid!" the blonde ordered.

Once more, disaster threatened. Josef, fearing what the Germans might do to Stefania if she refused to go, again talked about fighting to the death. Stefania shook her head.

Packing a suitcase, she dressed Helena in her good clothes and talked cheerfully to the nurses about how much she looked forward to going. When the bus arrived, the nurses boarded, and the driver began beeping for Stefania. But she just strolled away, calling, "I've changed my mind—I'm not going. *Auf Wiedersehen!*"

The nurses shouted threats, but the driver, anxious to get away, drove off. Laughing, Stefania ran back to the house and threw her arms around Josef. "If they tried to take me, I would have socked them with one of your uppercuts!" she said.

Soon the whine of artillery shells filled the streets. One morning, on sentry duty, Josef called, "Germans coming!"

Three bedraggled members of the once-victorious *Wehrmacht* staggered wearily down Tatarska Street. It was the last glimpse of the Nazi enemy.

Finally, when they were sure they were safe, the 13 emaciated fugitives descended the ladder from the attic and spilled onto the street. "Germans gone!" said Josef with a laugh.

Joyful smiles spread from face to face. As the residents of 3 Tatarska Street embraced, Josef hugged Helena close, and then wrapped his arms around her heroic sister for an even longer embrace.

In 1945, a few months after the war ended, Josef Burzminski proposed to Stefania Podgorska. "You asked to stay one night," she teased him. "Now you want to make it a lifetime?"

In 1961 the couple immigrated to the United States, where Josef established a dental practice outside Boston, and they raised a son and daughter. Helena Podgorska married, became a doctor and practices in Wroclaw, Poland.

In 1993 Stefania and Josef took part in the dedication of the U.S. Holocaust Memorial Museum in Washington, D.C., along with the heads of state of Israel, Poland, the United States and many other countries. It was a reminder that, in the midst of the greatest evil man can inflict, great good is possible too.

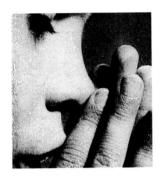

He does not believe that does not live

according to his belief.

THOMAS FULLER, M.D.

MY ONLY PRAYER

BY

LEE MAYNARD

We are hunkered down at the base of a rock overhang, the summit far above us, watching the rain fall softly. We are tired from climbing and running from the rain.

My 11-year-old grandson, Tristan, is with me. He knows about Martian landings and cyberspace, and just when you think that's all he is—an interesting child of a technological age—he names the Greek gods and tells how the citizens prayed to them.

"Maybe we should pray for a way out of here," I say, watching the rain grow heavier.

"Does prayer really work?" he asks. "Would it really get us out of here?"

I think carefully about what to say next . . . for I am not a prayerful man.

I have had my share of hurts and pains in the wilderness. The stings of scorpions. The snapping of bones. Dehydration so severe my eyes stung. But I never prayed over any of that. I always thought, if I put myself into those places, it was up to me to get out. God probably wasn't interested.

Prayer, I have always thought, was the thing you saved for last. But every time I got to the last, there was no time for praying. And when it was over, all I could do was wonder that I was still alive.

And so I never prayed. Except once.

It was 1978. In the early hours, when the tops of the trees were still lost in darkness, I parked my truck and stepped into New Mexico's Gila Wilderness. My plan was to hike 20 miles in, then join up with a group of nine Outward Bound School students and their instructors, a "patrol." I was the school director, and I was worried about this patrol: three New England preppies, a college freshman, three high-school graduates from Dallas, and two South Chicago street kids who had been sentenced to Outward Bound in lieu of jail.

I looked forward to hiking in the Gila. Even after half a lifetime spent outdoors, I couldn't seem to see it enough. But it was midsummer, and the sun's heat poured down relentlessly. At midday I stopped, drank some water and for the first time noticed the heat in my boots.

The boots were not new. I had worn them for some weeks and thought they were ready for the Gila. I was wrong.

I tried everything for relief: stopped and aired my feet, put on extra socks, quickened my pace, slowed my pace, tightened the laces, applied moleskin. Nothing worked.

I reached camp in the middle of the evening meal, took off my boots and socks, and padded around on the soft forest floor. I inspected my feet and counted 11 blisters, near blisters and hot spots. Still, I told no one about my problem.

We sat and talked for hours. After two weeks in the wilderness, only one student, a New Englander, seemed disenchanted with the course. He had tried to quit, but had been talked out of it by the staff.

In the morning the New Englander was gone. He had left hours before, thrashing back down the trail I'd come in on. We couldn't just

let him go into the unforgiving wilderness. Since I was the extra man, I put on the devil boots and went after him.

I soon realized I wasn't just limping—I was walking as though barefoot on hot glass. As I shuffled and stumbled, I tried to keep my mind above my ankles. Again, nothing worked.

A new sound sucked its way into my consciousness, and I realized it was coming from my boots. I sat on a fallen tree, held my feet out in front of me and looked at the crimson oozing from the eyelets. If I took the boots off, I would never get them on again.

Eventually the trail came out of the brush and straight into the Gila River, flowing down from the high country through shaded canyons. By the time it got to me, this narrow, shallow river was still icy, and I couldn't wait to feel it against my baking feet. But when the water poured into my boots, the burning sensation was replaced with a thousand stabs that seemed to puncture every blister.

My scream cut through the canyon, and I went face forward into the water. Then I got up and staggered across the river.

Since there was no rational solution to my problem, my mind began to create irrational ones. The answer, obviously, was . . . a horse. If I just had a horse, my feet would no longer be a problem, and I could catch the New Englander.

Like King Richard III, I began to implore, "Give me another horse! Have mercy!" What was the next word? Oh, yes. "Jesu."

I knew I had only another hundred or so paces in me, and then I would stop, sit and wait. I'd probably see no one for days.

The sun was low against my back, and my shadow reached far down the stony trail. I would never get to the end of my shadow. And then I stopped.

The right shoulder of my shadow moved, a bulging darkness down on the trail. A huge mass, motionless now, blocked most of the low sun, an elongated head bobbing up in attention to my presence.

It was a horse. A ghost born of pain.

God, I thought, *the mind is an amazing thing*. It was a beautiful ghost, but I would have to make it go away. So I confronted it directly, dragging myself right up to the horse and grabbing its halter.

It was a real horse.

The animal had a halter and a lead rope but no saddle. Something was going on here that I didn't understand, but I was not going to question it. I gathered up the lead rope and struggled onto the horse's back. "A horse, a horse," I mumbled as it calmly carried me down the trail and into the falling darkness. "Jesu."

The horse walked through the night and did not stop until we got to the trailhead, where I found the New Englander sitting on the bumper of my truck. I took off the hated boots, bandaged my feet and hobbled the horse in a patch of grass. The New Englander and I slept nearby.

At first light two wranglers showed up looking for the horse, said it had never wandered off before, didn't know why it did this time. They said the horse's name was King.

The rain turns to sleet, and I think maybe Tristan and I will have to sleep out the storm on a mountain where there are no horses. He leans against me, and he is smiling.

"Did you really pray?" he asks. "For a horse?"

"Well . . . I was a little out of it. Mumbling. I'm not sure anything I said would qualify as a prayer."

"I think you did pray," he says. "And you got what you prayed for, and it scared you." As usual, he's gotten to the heart of the matter.

The sleet disappears, and a thick mist suffuses the mountain. But behind the mist is a bright light, glowing first silver and then gold.

"I did, didn't I?" I admitted. "I *did* pray."

We leave the overhang and start down the mountain, the air thick with the nectar of after-storm. It is one of the best days of my life.

Prayer still mystifies me. Maybe I shouldn't save it for last.

Faith furnishes prayer with wings, without which it cannot soar to Heaven.

SAINT JOHN CLIMACUS

"I STILL SEE HIM EVERYWHERE"

BY
RICHARD MORSILLI, WITH JO COUDERT

On February 22, 1983, young Todd Morsilli of Warwick, Rhode Island, was struck and killed by a drunk driver. He was one of 19,500 Americans who lost their lives that year in accidents caused by intoxicated drivers. That fall, Todd's father was asked to speak to students at Riverdale Country School, just north of Manhattan, about teenage drunk driving.

As he looked around the assembly hall, Richard Morsilli wondered what he could say to persuade the students to listen. They seemed bored, restless. He felt he couldn't lecture. All he really wanted to do was to tell them how much he missed Todd. Which, more or less, is what he did.

His talk, interspersed with his thoughts as he addressed the teenagers, follows.

Good morning. My name is Richard Morsilli. Eight months ago my son Todd was struck and killed by a 17-year-old drunk driver. Todd was 13. He was a wonderful boy.

Why did I say he was wonderful? Every father thinks his kid is special. But Todd really was. He had a knack of making people feel good about themselves. The day before he was killed, I heard him say to Carole, "Hey, Mom, my friends think you're pretty."

Todd was a tennis player. He was ranked No. 3 in his age group in New England in singles, No. 1 in doubles. He was also a baseball player, and when he was younger that's all he cared about, even after we got a tennis court. Then one day his older brother had no one to play with and persuaded Todd to pick up a racket. In six months Todd was winning tournaments.

That's what made us so close, my driving him to tournaments, and having all that time in the car together. That fellow in the third row with the sun-bleached hair has the same thoughtful look Todd would get when we'd discuss things.

It sounds like Todd was really competitive, but he wasn't. I'd say, "Todd, how will you play this guy? I hear he's got a terrific cross-court return." And he'd say, "Gee, Dad, I don't know. I haven't thought about it." He liked to win, but he didn't much like to beat people. His coach urged him to play older kids to sharpen his skills, but he hated to do it because he knew it upset them to get beaten by a youngster.

I was the one who had visions of Wimbledon. All Todd ever said was, "That's a long way off, Dad. A lot can happen." Did he sense what was coming, like the garden that blooms like crazy just before frost?

Last February 22, Todd was walking along the street with his cousin Jeff. The two boys were only five weeks apart in age, and inseparable. Jeff had been watching Todd play tennis that morning, and they were on their way to rent skis for a Catholic Youth Organization weekend. First they stopped at our house to get money for ice-cream cones. "You know, Mom," Todd said after she had given him what change she had in her pocketbook, "what we'd really like are milk shakes." His mother laughed and went upstairs for more money.

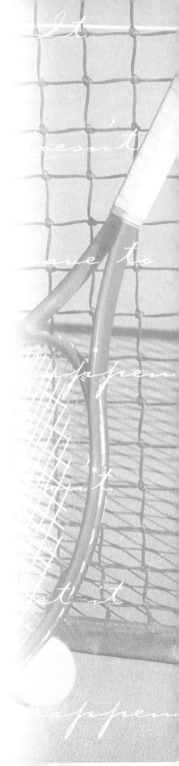

That girl in the third row with the sweet face just caught her breath. She's thinking what Carole can't help but think—that if she'd said no, the boys would have left the house earlier; they'd have turned the corner before the car came.

An elderly neighbor told us afterward that he was out shoveling his driveway when the boys went by. It was a holiday, Washington's Birthday, and the sun sparkling on the snow made the world seem paved with diamonds. The boys offered to finish the job for him, but he said he was glad to be outside, and they went on. The neighbor saw the car coming. Jeff saw it too. The car was weaving. They both shouted and Jeff jumped into a snowbank, but Todd . . . Todd . . . couldn't get out of the way.

Oh, God, help me get through this without crying. I've got to keep going.

The car . . . struck Todd. He was . . . thrown 90 feet. . . . The car didn't stop . . .

It's been eight months. Will I ever be able to talk about it without breaking down?

I'm sorry. Forgive me. You just can't imagine how . . . overwhelming it is. I got a call at my office. It was someone at the hospital. The voice said a boy's been hurt. We think it's your son. Can you come right away? All I remember is saying, over and over: Just let there be a chance. He'll make it, if he has a chance, because he doesn't give up.

He didn't get his chance. At the hospital a priest met me and took me into a little room. . . . Todd's mother and I didn't even have time to hope. By the time we knew about it all, he was gone.

He's gone, and I still see him everywhere. I see him as I glance around this hall. In the clean line of your chin, there on the aisle. And there, first row middle, in your slim, strong frame. And in you, too, young lady, in the way he bit his lip to keep the tears from coming.

The next thing you know you're preparing for a funeral. You're saying things like: His grave's got to be under a tree. You're making telephone calls. You're answering the doorbell. His friends . . .

Little girls asking if they could have one of Todd's tennis shirts. Little boys intending just to shake hands, but then moving into my arms as though, if we hugged hard enough, we could blot out the emptiness.

Nine hundred people jammed the church for his funeral. "It was like he was everyone's best friend," a 15-year-old who spoke at the service said. "You were just glad he was your friend too."

We buried Todd in his warm-up suit and his cap. Everyone knew that beige-felt cap. It was like the one worn by Frew McMillan, the South African tennis player. Todd admired him because he was always a gentleman on court.

Afterward, we got letters from all over the country—hundreds of letters—from people who'd met Todd at tournaments. They pretty much said the same thing: We knew your son. He was a terrific tennis player. But, even more, he was such a nice boy.

I called one father to ask if his son Andrew, a black friend of Todd's, would be a pallbearer. "Andrew would really like that," his father said. "He thought the world of your boy, ever since the first time they played a match against each other. Andrew had forgotten his water bottle, and Todd leaned over and said, 'Share mine.'"

A black boy, a Chinese boy and two Jewish boys, his tennis rivals and friends, helped carry Todd to his grave. They followed everyone else up to the altar for communion.

Then the funeral was over. You've buried your son, and you go back to work. The world goes on. But things don't mean the same. I'm no different from your fathers. I wanted to provide a bright future for my family. All I can tell you now is I'd give up all I have in a minute if I could just have Todd back.

Shall I tell them about the fox? No, probably not. I don't want them to turn me off.

Because of Todd's tennis playing, there was a lot in the newspapers about the tragedy. They called it a hit-and-run accident, which it was, except that the girl ran into a tree a mile down the road so the police caught her right away. She'd spent the holiday drinking beer at a friend's house, starting at ten in the morning, and later they switched to vodka.

If you wish to strive for peace of soul and pleasure, then believe.

HEINRICH HEINE

She goes to school. I see her at the supermarket. Is her life going on as usual? Did Todd's death make any difference?

People wanted to do something. They started a Todd Morsilli Memorial Fund. Somebody suggested renaming the tennis courts at Roger Williams Park in Providence in honor of Todd. In June the first annual Todd Morsilli Memorial Tournament was held there.

Sometimes I tell myself: He was just a 13-year-old boy. How could he have touched so many lives? Sometimes I think: It was just another tragedy. How could so many lives be so terribly changed by it? But it's true.

I worry about Todd's brother, David. He looks so much like Todd that people expect him to *be* Todd. I worry about Todd's sister Lisa, because she and Todd were closest. I worry about Todd's kid sister Kristin. She was visiting a friend before the accident and hadn't seen Todd in two days. She's recently become very enthusiastic about tennis. Is she genuinely interested? Or is she trying to make up to us for Todd? And I worry about Jeff, Todd's cousin, because he lost his father four months before Todd was killed.

I pray every day he'll make it. I pray every day that all of us make it.

They say grief brings people closer together. It's not true. Grief is isolating. It locks you up in your own heart. If Carole and I hadn't had such a good marriage, I think we'd have come apart. I was out of the house all day, but Carole was home, and everywhere she looked there was something to remind her of Todd. And I think the strain began to tell.

What saved us was the squirrel. If Kristin hadn't told Carole about the car in front of us hitting a squirrel and my getting out, pointlessly, to move the poor broken body to the side of the road and then sitting down on the curb sobbing, the silence might have won out over us. But that squirrel saved Carole and me. We talked to each other then. We realized we had to get help, and Carole took a part-time job to get out of the house.

I'm not on a crusade. As you know by now, I'm no speaker. And I didn't come to tell you not to drink. I only came to say that when you do drink, please, *please*, don't drive. If you're with someone who's drinking, please, *please*, call your parents to come get you. Because if something happens to you, it won't be just another tragedy; it'll be their beloved child. And if you kill someone else's child, it'll be someone like my son Todd. It doesn't have to happen. Don't let it happen.

I guess that's all I have to say. Thank you for listening.

Did I say enough? Did I say too much? Why, they're applauding. They're all standing up. That fellow is coming up on the platform. He's holding out his hand. They're lining up. Are they all going to shake my hand?

Thank you. I'm glad I came too. No, she didn't go to jail. Her three-year sentence was suspended. Her probation terms included regular psychological counseling, work at a halfway house and no drinking. And her driver's license was suspended for five years.

Thank you. Take care of yourselves. All of you, please, *please*, take care of yourselves.

What nice kids they are. I think if I'd told them about the fox, they'd have understood. They'd have appreciated how astonishing it was, when we'd never seen a fox before, to have one come and stand on the patio two days after Todd's death—just come and stand there staring at the kitchen window before it turned and slowly moved away.

Carole's pregnant sister came to be with her that afternoon. "I've been looking at a book of baby names," she said. "Did you know when you named Todd that it means 'fox'?"

Was Todd trying to tell us he's all right? I think these kids would understand how much we want to believe that.

Faith is the bird that sings when the dawn
is still dark.

RABINDRANATH TAGORE

TEST OF FAITH

BY

BRYAN SMITH

A slight chill bit the night air as Wes Anderson climbed into his silver sedan. It was 8:30 on March 7, 1994, and the burly 34-year-old minister of Carmichael Christian Church in Sacramento, California, had just finished a meeting with several church members.

"Have a good evening, Pastor," a member of his congregation called out.

"I will," Wes answered. Then chiding gently in his Tennessee twang, he added, "Hope to see y'all Sunday."

Wes had been studying criminal justice in college when he felt a call to the church. He came to Carmichael in 1992, and the 110-member congregation responded warmly to the easygoing man with the broad smile.

Driving home, Wes saw one of his congregants, 78-year-old Dorothy Hearst, locked in a three-car fender bender. Wes stopped to help, and was relieved that she was only slightly shaken. Suddenly, fast-approaching headlights flashed toward them. "Dorothy!" Wes shouted. "He's going to hit us!" Wes shoved her out of the way just as a station wagon slammed into his right side, crushing him against Hearst's car. His right leg exploded in pain. Then he lay writhing on the asphalt, his right leg nearly severed.

As the ambulance arrived at the University of California, Davis, Medical Center, a doctor thrust a surgical consent form into the pastor's hand. "There's no other way to say this," he said. "Your right leg may have to be amputated."

Shortly after the surgery, Wes felt an agonizing cramp gnarled in his right calf. He reached down to rub the area, but recoiled. There was nothing there.

Phantom pain—physical sensation experienced by amputees when the brain signals that the limb is still there—would come and go like torturing ghosts. Each time, he winced from the sharp, shooting pangs in the leg that was no longer there. All of this because of James Allen Napier—a drunken driver who would spend only eight months in jail.

As the days wore on, Wes fell into depression. Surgeries left his remaining leg raked with scars. Red welts crisscrossed his stomach, a road map where tissue for skin grafts had been taken.

"It isn't fair," he complained to Mike Cook, his friend and the pastor of Carmichael Christian's sister church, Sylvan Oaks. "I wanted to have a wife and children someday. What woman could love me with all these injuries and scars?"

"Life isn't fair," Mike replied. "But is it supposed to be? You've seen terrible things happen to good people. Remember, Wes, you saved a life. I know it's hard to believe, but God has his reasons."

Wes looked away. He, too, counseled his flock to keep the faith in times of trouble. "God always has a plan," he had told them. "Trust his will." But the words he once thought so powerful suddenly seemed so small.

A reporter from the Sacramento *Bee* called, wanting to tell his story. Wes's instinct was to say no; he didn't want to be portrayed as a hero. The reporter promised to simply recount what happened, and Wes finally gave in. *Who knows,* he thought. *Maybe it could do someone some good.*

Virginia Bruegger dropped the March 16, 1994, Sacramento *Bee* on a pile by her bed. As usual, making it through the day had been a scramble. First her car wouldn't start; then she missed the bus. For the past year and a half, the 38-year-old divorced mother had adopted a relentless schedule of classes, study and internships to earn a bachelor's degree in behavioral science at the University of California, Davis. Now, as midterms loomed in her last year, her shoestring budget was stretched to the limit.

Just as she settled in at her kitchen table that night to study, her 16-year-old son, Steven, became sick from food poisoning. At 3 a.m. Virginia trudged to her room, exhausted. Suddenly the pressure felt crushing. *Am I doing the right thing?* she wondered. *Will I be able to find a job after graduation?*

A newspaper headline jumped out at her: "Pastor Loses Leg Saving Woman from Car Crash." She lifted the section and began reading.

My God, she thought, *what this man went through.* Virginia stopped at the quote the pastor gave as his reason for telling his story—that it might help get "people's lives spiritually on track."

It's as if he's speaking directly to me, she thought. Virginia had had a religious upbringing in the small town of Bushton, Kansas. But since her divorce she'd drifted away from her faith; until now she could barely recollect a prayer.

As the morning sunlight arrived, classes loomed just hours away. *Not today,* Virginia thought. Something told her she had to meet this man.

Awakening from his seventh surgery in ten days, Wes didn't know what to make of the woman at his door with a potted ivy plant in her hand. Her sparkling brown eyes registered a shy look until she smiled—then her whole face brightened.

"I just wanted to thank you," Virginia began, groping for words. *What do I say to him?* she wondered. Dozens of cards crowded a bedside stand and clung to a wall next to the bed. Flowers sent by friends, family and Wes's congregation bloomed in every corner. His story had obviously touched many people, not just her.

"I read the article in the paper, and I had to let you know what your story did for me," Virginia said. "It changed my perspective on what I've been going through. I've been having kind of a tough time."

Do I sound whiny? she wondered. *This man, after all, has gone through a real trial—not just a few worries over bills and school.* Wes's expression reassured her. "Your story helped me realize that I needed to get my relationship back on track with the Lord."

Wes studied this stranger. Since he'd been in the hospital, Wes had barely had a moment free of pain. Now his mind was less on himself and more on how he could help. "Do you have a church?" he asked.

Virginia shook her head. Such a simple thing. *He got right to the problem,* she thought, and reached out to shake his hand. Wes took it, but he pulled away a little quickly. *I hope I haven't been too forward,* she thought.

Wes hadn't meant to draw back. It was instinct; he still felt wounded, and he was exhausted. Funny, though, her thanking him. For some reason it was he who felt better.

Within a week of meeting Wes, Virginia found a church near her home and sent Wes a note. She then visited him a second time two weeks later; they compared notes about their lives. They discussed her classes and job prospects, and talked about how his physical therapy was coming along.

He's so easy to talk to, Virginia mused on her way home. Every few days, she'd send him a note or drop by.

About two months after the accident, Virginia phoned Wes. "I'm being discharged today!" he said, his voice barely able to contain his excitement.

After they hung up, Virginia was struck by an inexplicable feeling. She hopped in her car and sped to the medical center.

"What are you doing here?" Wes asked, revealing his surprise.

"I'm not sure," Virginia replied, a bit shakily. "I just felt like I was supposed to be here."

"Well, I'm glad you are," he said, smiling.

As they approached his small A-frame church, Wes's eyes began to fill. On a black wrought-iron fence, dozens of yellow ribbons blossomed like bright flowers. Children from the church's elementary school jumped up and down, waving at his car. Banners proclaimed: "We love you! Welcome home, Mr. Anderson!"

Virginia felt tears too.

In June, wearing a cap and gown, Virginia strode proudly down an auditorium aisle and accepted her degree. Unable to attend because of church obligations, Wes had sent congratulatory flowers. A few nights later, the two friends and their parents met for dinner. They had much in common. Both of their parents had been married for more than 40 years; they were both raised in the Methodist Church.

"You even talk like me!" Wes chided.

"I may have a drawl," Virginia kidded back, "but I'm not that bad."

As a coal is revived by incense, prayer revives the hope of the heart.

J. W. VON GOETHE

At home, Wes finished buttoning his shirt as he was getting ready to go to church. Suddenly he felt himself falling backward toward the floor. He landed directly on his stump and screamed in agony. Wes spent the next nine days in bed. He'd always prided himself on being independent, strong. Now, doubt and depression crashed over him.

He even began to question his relationship with Virginia. "I really like her," Wes told Mike. "I'm just worried that this might be some sympathy thing. I mean, I was never a Hollywood star, but look at me now."

"Wes, you're not any less of a person than you were before the accident," Mike said. "What's important is what's on the inside."

It had been several days since Virginia had heard from Wes. She thought about their last meeting, a visit to Muir Woods National Monument. *Did I do something wrong?* Virginia wondered. They had talked openly about her divorce eight years ago and her struggle to make a better life for herself and Steven. When she'd been out with other men, she'd worried where things were leading. With Wes such things never crossed her mind. *He's different from any man I've ever known,* Virginia thought.

When Wes finally called, he asked Virginia to the state fair and surprised her by picking her up in his car, newly adapted for the loss of his leg. Under a star-filled sky they sat and watched the fireworks display. "I was starting to wonder when I'd see you again," Virginia said.

"I'm sorry," Wes replied. "It's just that I don't do a lot of dating. If I go out with someone, I look on it as something serious. I treasure your friendship, and I'd never want to jeopardize it. I just . . ."

Virginia interrupted. "Wes, before you go any further . . ."

Wes looked down. *This is the part where she'll say let's just be friends.*

"You need to know I care about you as an individual," Virginia continued, "and not whether you have one leg or two. To me, you are a whole man, a complete person."

Wes listened, stunned. "I love you," he said, his voice thick with emotion.

"I love you too," Virginia replied. For the first time, they kissed.

That Easter, Wes and Virginia helped set up a sunrise service outdoors. Wes struggled through wet grass with his artificial leg and lost his balance. He slammed to the ground, feeling the old flames of anger, frustration and doubt.

Virginia rushed to his side, but Wes didn't look up, afraid of what he might see. *Fear? Pity?* He'd never doubted her, but he felt so vulnerable. A grown man, helpless.

At that moment the truth dawned on him. *I've focused on the outside, when it was my inside that really needed to heal.*

Virginia and a friend helped Wes up. He was shaken and embarrassed. But at last he wasn't afraid. *This is who I am,* he realized. *A man who will fall occasionally, but who will rise, each time stronger.*

On May 27, 1995, Wes came in through a side door to the altar of the Carmichael Christian Church, dressed in a white tuxedo and gripping a black cane. He looked to the entrance as Virginia, in a beaded white gown, came toward him, escorted by her parents.

The church was full as Mike Cook performed the wedding ceremony. "Two are better than one," Mike said, reading from Ecclesiastes. "If one falls down, his friend can help him up. But pity the man who falls and has no one to help him up."

As the service ended, Wes stood before a flight of stairs leading to the congregation. Holding hands with Virginia, he walked down, step by step, until they reached the bottom.

A little more than a year before, Wes had wondered about God's plan. Now he knew.

If the stars should appear just one night in

a thousand years, how would men believe

and adore!

RALPH WALDO EMERSON

"I DIED AT 10:52 A.M."

BY

VICTOR D. SOLOW

When I left home with my wife that fine spring day to go for a ten-minute jog, I did not know that I would be gone for two weeks. My trip was the one that all of us must make eventually, from which only a rare few return. In my case a series of events occurred so extraordinarily timed to allow my eventual survival that words like "luck" or "coincidence" no longer seem applicable.

It was a beautiful Saturday morning. We had jogged and were driving back home to Mamaroneck, New York, along the Boston Post Road. It was 10:52 a.m. I had just stopped at a red light, opposite a gas station. My long, strange trip was about to start, and I must now use my wife's words to describe what happened for the next few minutes:

"Victor turned to me and said, 'Oh, Lucy, I . . .' Then, as swiftly as the expiration of a breath, he seemed simply to settle down in his seat with all his weight. His head remained erect, his eyes opened wide, like someone utterly astonished. I knew instantly he could no longer hear or see me.

"I pulled on the emergency brake, pleading with him to hang on, shouting for help. The light changed and traffic moved around my car. No one noticed me. My husband's color had now turned gray-green; his mouth hung open, but his eyes continued seemingly to view an astounding scene. I frantically tried to pull him to the other seat so I could drive him to the hospital. Then my cries for help attracted Frank Colangelo, proprietor of the gas station, who telephoned the police."

It was now 10:55—three minutes had elapsed since my heart arrest. A first-aid manual reads, "When breathing and heartbeat stop and are not artificially started, death is inevitable. Therefore, artificial resuscitation must be started immediately. Seconds count." Time was running out. In another 60 seconds my brain cells could start to die.

Now came the first of the coincidences: Before police headquarters could radio the emergency call, Officer James Donnellan, cruising along the Boston Post Road, arrived at the intersection where our car seemed stalled. Checking me for pulse and respiration, and finding neither, he pulled me from the car with the help of Mr. Colangelo, and immediately started cardiopulmonary resuscitation.

In the meantime, the police alert had reached Officer Michael Sena, who chanced to be cruising just half a mile from the scene. He reached me in less than half a minute. From his car Sena yanked an oxygen tank and an apparatus with a mask used to force air into the lungs. Within seconds he had the mask over my face. Donnellan continued with heart massage. Sena later told me, "I was sure we were just going through the motions. I would have bet my job that you were gone."

Police headquarters also alerted the emergency rescue squad via a high-pitched radio signal on the small alert boxes all squad members carry on their belts. When his warning signal went off, Tom McCann, volunteer fireman and trained emergency medical technician, was conducting a fire inspection. He looked up and saw Officers Donnellan and Sena working on a "body" less than 50 yards away. McCann made the right connection and raced over, arriving just ten seconds after his alarm sounded.

"I tried the carotid pulse—you had no pulse," McCann later said. "There was no breathing. Your eyes were open, and your pupils were dilated—a bad sign!" Dilated pupils indicate that blood is not reaching the brain. It can mean that death has occurred.

It was 10:56. McCann, who weighs 270 pounds, began to give me a no-nonsense heart massage.

The strange coincidences continued. The emergency-squad warning beeper went off at the exact moment when Peter Brehmer, Ronald Capasso, Chip Rigano, and Richard and Paul Torpey were meeting at the firehouse to change shifts. A moment later and they would have left. The ambulance was right there. Everybody piled in. Manned by five trained first-aid technicians, the ambulance arrived three minutes later. It was 10:59.

When I was being moved into the ambulance, United Hospital in Port Chester, six miles distant, was radioed. The hospital called a "Code 99" over its loudspeaker system, signaling all available personnel into the Emergency Room. Here, an ideal combination of specialists was available: when I arrived, two internists, two surgeons, two technicians from the cardiology department, two respiratory therapists and four nurses were waiting. Doctor Harold Roth later said: "The patient at that point was dead by available standards. There was no measurable pulse, he was not breathing, and he appeared to have no vital signs whatever."

11:10 a.m. A cardiac monitor was attached; a tube supplying pure oxygen was placed in my windpipe; intravenous injections were started. An electric-shock apparatus was then attached to my chest.

11:14. The first electric shock was powerful enough to lift my body inches off the operating table. But there was no result; my heart still showed no activity.

11:15. A second electric shock was applied—a final try. Twenty-three minutes had elapsed since my heart had stopped. Now, excitement exploded around the operating table as an irregular heart rhythm suddenly showed on the monitor. To everyone's amazement, I sat bolt upright and started to get off the table. I had to be restrained.

Sometime later I was aware that my eyes were open. But I was still part of another world. It seemed that by chance I had been given this human body and it was difficult to wear. Doctor Roth later related: "I came to see you in the Coronary Care Unit. You were perfectly conscious. I asked how you felt, and your response was: 'I feel like I've been there and I've come back.' It was true: you were there and now you were back."

A hard time followed. I could not connect with the world around me. Was I really here now, or was it an illusion? Was that other condition of being I had just experienced the reality, or was *that* the illusion? I would lie there and observe my body with suspicion and amazement. It seemed to be doing things of its own volition and I was a visitor within. How strange to see my hand reach out for something. Eating, drinking, watching people had a dreamlike, slow-motion quality as if seen through a veil.

During those first few days I was two people. My absent-mindedness and strange detachment gave the doctors pause. Perhaps the brain had been damaged after all. Their concern is reflected in hospital records: "Retrograde amnesia and difficulty with subsequent current events was recognized . . . .The neurologist felt prognosis was rather guarded regarding future good judgment . . ."

On the sixth day there was a sudden change. When I woke up, the world around me no longer seemed so peculiar. Something in me had decided to complete the return trip. From that day on, recovery was rapid. Eight days later I was discharged from the hospital.

Now family, friends and strangers began to ask what "death was like." Could I remember what had happened during those 23 minutes when heart and breathing stopped? I found that the experience could not easily be communicated.

Later, feeling and thinking my way back into the experience, I discovered why I could not make it a simple recital of events: when I left my body I also left all sensory human tools behind with which we perceive the world we take for real. But I found that I now *knew* certain things about my place in this world and my relationship to that other reality. My knowing was not through my brain but with another part of me which I cannot explain.

Blessed are those who have not seen, and yet believe.

JOHN 20

For me, the moment of transition from life to death—what else can one call it?—was easy. There was no time for fear, pain or thought. There was no chance "to see my whole life before me," as others have related. The last impression I can recall lasted a brief instant. I was moving at high speed toward a net of great luminosity. The strands and knots where the luminous lines intersected were vibrating with a tremendous cold energy. The grid appeared as a barrier that would prevent further travel. I did not want to move through the grid. For a brief moment my speed appeared to slow down. Then I was in the grid. The instant I made contact with it, the vibrant luminosity increased to a blinding intensity which drained, absorbed and transformed me at the same time. There was no pain. The sensation was neither pleasant nor unpleasant but completely consuming. The nature of everything had changed. Words only vaguely approximate the experience from this instant on.

The grid was like a transformer, an energy converter transporting me through form and into formlessness, beyond time and space. Now I was not in a place, nor even in a dimension, but rather in a condition of being. This new "I" was not the I which I knew, but rather a distilled essence of it, yet something vaguely familiar, something I had always known buried under a superstructure of personal fears, hopes, wants and needs. This "I" had no connection to ego. It was final, unchangeable, indivisible, indestructible pure spirit. While completely unique and individual as a fingerprint, "I" was, at the same time, part of some infinite, harmonious and ordered whole. I had been there before.

The condition "I" was in was pervaded by a sense of great stillness and deep quiet. Yet there was also a sense of something momentous about to be revealed, a further change. But there is nothing further to tell except of my sudden return to the operating table.

I would like to repeat that these experiences outside the dimensions of our known reality did not "happen" as if I were on some sort of a voyage I could recollect. Rather, I discovered them afterward, rooted in my consciousness as a kind of unquestionable knowing. Being of a somewhat skeptical turn of mind, I am willing to grant the possibility that this is a leftover of some subtle form of brain damage. I know, however, that since my return from that other condition of being, many of my attitudes toward our world have changed and continue to change, almost by themselves. A recurrent nostalgia remains for that other reality, that condition of indescribable stillness and quiet where the "I" is part of a harmonious whole. The memory softens the old drives for possession, approval and success.

I have just returned from a pleasant, slow, mile-and-a-half jog. I am sitting in our garden writing. Overhead a huge dogwood moves gently in a mild southerly breeze. Two small children, holding hands, walk down the street absorbed in their own world. I am glad I am here and now. But I know that this marvelous place of sun and wind, flowers, children and lovers, this murderous place of evil, ugliness and pain, is only one of many realities through which I must travel to distant and unknown destinations. For the time being I belong to the world and it belongs to me.

You can keep a faith only as you can keep

a plant, by rooting it into your life and

making it grow there.

PHILLIPS BROOKS

PROGRESS OF A PILGRIM

BY

PRISCILLA BUCKLEY

One summer morning in 1985, my mother asked me to join her on a pilgrimage. Coming from Mom, it was no surprise. She went to Mass every morning and began each meal with grace. She was so religious, we used to tell our friends, she got memos from God.

I followed Mom's example as best I could. But I grew up in the turbulent 1960s, and my faith never kindled. I remember watching Mom during that endless Sunday hour between ten and 11, her brow pinched with devotion, and wondering, *What on earth does she see in it all?*

By the age of 15, I had stopped going to church—a fact that caused us no small tension. I thought it hypocritical to attend if I wasn't sincere. Mom thought I should come anyway. Coming meant you were halfway there, she said. Her words fell on deaf ears.

Over the years Mom and I became as close as sea and shore, but we could never discuss religion. We put the subject away, a dangling conversation we both knew we must someday conclude.

That time had not yet come when Mom asked me to break away from work to accompany her to a small town in Yugoslavia—Medjugorje. A pilgrimage? In my case, certainly not. But I'd never been to that part of the world. In October 1985, we went.

Medjugorje, in southern Bosnia and Herzegovina, is in hill country. For generations, people there had farmed tobacco and grapes, herded scrawny goats and eked out a living.

Then in June 1981, on one of those hills, six village children saw what they later would describe as a bright light shaped like a woman. "The Gospa!" stammered one of the girls. It was the Croatian name for the Virgin Mary.

The children claimed that the vision appeared to them at the same hour each evening, saying she had come to show the way to peace. Their story understandably met a wall of doubt. Yugoslavia's Communist authorities harassed their families, threatening them with the loss of work unless they silenced the children.

The church also expressed doubts. The parish priest, Father Jozo Zovko, counseled his flock to remain skeptical. But one day while he was praying for a sign of what to do, an inner voice told him, "Protect the children." Just then the children rushed in, saying the militia was after them. The priest hid them. Later when authorities ordered him to put an end to the crowded evening Masses, he refused.

Finally the militia arrested Father Jozo. He was kept in solitary confinement in an unheated cell for a year and a half. When released, he was forbidden to resume parish duties in Medjugorje. But the priest's removal from the parish did nothing to stem the growing religious fervor.

Soon, pilgrims were flocking to Medjugorje from around the world. By the time we arrived, millions had already visited the place.

During the week Mom and I stayed in Medjugorje, I went to Mass with her daily. We elbowed through swarms of pilgrims and joined the crowds straining to glimpse the children.

53

At week's end, Mom was flush with exhilaration in her renewed faith. I was dizzy with relief at being able to go home. Once back, I shut the door to Medjugorje behind me and resumed life as usual.

Some time after that, I met a theater director named Alain, and nine short months later we were married. Another 11 months and our son, Michael, was born. I found a job that paid more than I'd ever earned. We bought the house of our dreams and plunged into transforming it, hiring workmen, poring over catalogues. We worked hard all week and combed flea markets on weekends, our lives pulsing lustily to the rhythm of earn-and-spend, spend-and-earn.

While I pondered decorating decisions, Yugoslavia was plunged into the fiery caldron of ethnic war. The evening news broadcasts were dominated by images of once-bustling towns smoldering in ruins and roadsides strewn with corpses. What a mockery the war seemed to make of Medjugorje's message of peace!

One August evening Alain and I were bustling around our kitchen preparing a favorite dish. Everything was ready but the steamed vegetables. When I pried open the pressure-cooker lid, the pot blew up and plastered my face with scalding orange mash. I reeled back, thinking, *My face is on fire!* As I plunged my face in the kitchen sink and turned on the cold water, every nerve was screaming, *Take it away, take it away!*

I spent a long evening in excruciating pain at the hospital emergency room. After a cursory examination, the young intern casually pronounced there wasn't much he could do. He dropped a small white pill in my hand and ordered a nurse to apply some cream.

In the stillness that followed, my life dropped its party-dress veneer. Desperately—almost in reflex—I called out to God to help me. The only response was the steady throbbing of blistering flesh, and I felt a rising tide of despair.

For months afterward I flailed in anguish. My face was a grisly pastiche of varying shades of raw. Alain was patient and understanding, but

I was haunted by my appearance. People stared when I passed. I feared I'd be disfigured forever.

My mother called often, offering encouragement. Then one day she returned to the conversation we had never been able to finish. "Do you pray, honey?" she asked, almost hesitantly. "I'm sure it would help."

I said that I was trying but that every attempt had failed. Hanging up the phone, I longed for Mom's bedrock faith.

In time, my face healed. To get back on track, I saw the physical therapist, the ophthalmologist, the dermatologist. I focused on Alain and Michael and the everyday. But the anguish remained.

One day I drove to visit my cousin Michael, a monk in a Benedictine monastery. For hours we talked about the accident and my feeble efforts to put my life back together. Only when I was about to leave did he mention his own prayer life, which he called a "conversation with God."

The expression stayed with me on the ride home. I still had no idea how to begin, but I knew I wanted to. Perhaps, I reasoned, if I could go where God's presence was more evident, I would feel comfortable in praying. It was then that I was seized with the desire to return to Medjugorje—this time as a pilgrim in earnest.

Medjugorje in 1994 was a far cry from the sparse cluster of run-down red-roofed houses I'd visited almost a decade earlier. The houses had been repaired and spruced up. There was now a stone esplanade in front of the church, and taxis ferried people around.

Pilgrims were everywhere. By day they intoned prayers along the dirt paths of the village. Each evening they filled the seats at Mass. One day a woman plopped down next to me after Mass, training bright eyes on me like headlights on a deer. "What group are you with?" she inquired cheerfully. I told her I wasn't with any. "Oh, you poor thing! Maria! Dorothy! Come pray with this poor girl. She's all alone."

As the days crept by, however, I saw that beneath the loudspeaker displays of devotion, something was happening. The violent conflict among Croats, Muslims, and Serbs had shattered this region. Yet while villages all around it had been bombed and mortared, hardly a house in Medjugorje had been harmed, not an inhabitant hurt. And 13 years after first reporting the apparitions, five of the children, now adults, were still in the village, proclaiming the message of peace.

The day before I was to return home, I traveled to a hilltop monastery to visit Father Jozo Zovko, the priest who had protected the children. A slender figure in a brown robe, he had intense dark eyes that plumbed mine expectantly. "I've been here once before," I stammered. I explained how I'd had an accident, had foundered and had come back.

He nodded, pursing his mouth thoughtfully at his fingertips. "People who need help will go to the place where they can find it," he said. "The important thing is to come. Everything else will be given you."

The important thing is to come. The words, so like my mother's, haunted me as I traveled home to Alain and Michael. I thought of my life during the past ten years—a patchwork progression through marriage and motherhood, culminating in an ill-opened kitchen appliance. In that time, the peace of Medjugorje had continued, an oasis in the night. Like my mother's faith, it was still bearing fruit.

I go to church often now. Each time I step inside, the rich, familiar rites tell me it is good that I've come. My son, Michael, now five, accom-

There is not in the world a kind of life more sweet and delightful than that of a continual conversation with God.

NICHOLAS HERMAN OF LORRAINE
(BROTHER LAWRENCE)

56

panies me every now and again. He spends the time fidgeting and running up and down the aisles, no more interested in the proceedings than I was at his age.

One day I caught him looking at me with the same expression of bewilderment I used to shoot at my own mother. I couldn't help smiling.

Michael, wherever your path leads, you've already taken your first step toward God, I thought. *The important thing is to come.*

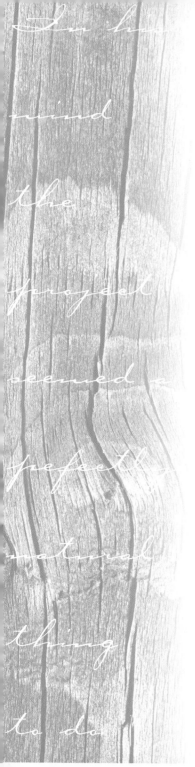

SILENT NIGHT

BY

BARBARA SANDE DIMMITT

German fighter planes wheeled through flak-littered air on February 21, 1944, cannons blazing at the U.S. bombers heading back to England. It was the eighth mission for U.S. Air Force pilot Clair Cline and the crew of his B-24 Liberator. Suddenly the plane's tail section shuddered. Cline looked at his instrument panel and saw the reflection of flames behind him. For a split second his thoughts were of his young wife, Anne, back home in Tacoma, Washington. Then he ordered, "Bail out!"

Two weeks later, Cline, along with his copilot, navigator and bombardier, arrived at Stalag Luft I, a prison camp in northern Germany. Snow still lay on the ground, and during those late-winter nights the crew, along with 12 other men in room 6, barrack 6, huddled in their bunks, freezing without adequate heat or blankets. For meals they had only barley with flecks that turned out to be weevils, bread fortified with sawdust, stew laced with shrapnel.

As spring arrived and the weather warmed, however, the worst problem for these men became boredom. They waited for news of the war, searching for ways to keep their minds off worries about loved ones.

58

Cline turned to his childhood hobby of model-building to pass the time. First he made an intricate replica of a B-24 out of scrap wood. Then one day as he strolled along the barbed-wire fence, he recalled how he'd once taken Anne to a concert by violinist Isaac Stern. Anne's blue eyes had sparkled at his virtuosity. Suddenly, Cline hit on a project that might distract him from the miseries of prison camp.

"Hey, what're you doing?" asked Ed Wenrich, a barrack mate. For the past 20 minutes Cline had been carrying a bed slat from bunk to bunk, comparing it with the other wooden crosspieces.

"I want to swap my slats for some with matching grains," Cline said, peering under a mattress. "I'm going to make a violin."

"You've gone around the bend for sure," said Cline's bombardier. "What are you going to use for tools?"

"I have a small pocketknife," said Cline, who had obtained it from the German guards by trading cigarettes, "and I'll grind a table knife on a rock to make a chisel. I can use a piece of broken glass for fine scraping." Ignoring the men's skeptical looks, Cline went back to work.

In his mind the project seemed a perfectly natural thing to do. Watching his father repair items on their farm had taught him ingenuity and patience. Cline had inherited a love of music from his mother, who played the accordion and told stories of her grandfather, a violinist in Denmark.

One day as a child, he spied a dusty violin case at his uncle's house. "I never could play that thing," said his uncle. "Do you want it?"

"Sure!" Cline exclaimed. Soon he was playing at dances. He found a book on the construction of stringed instruments. Neighbors began bringing him broken violins to fix.

Now, in this prison camp, he would make his own. After hunting through the barracks, Cline settled on a pair of beech bed slats for the

back of the violin and two pine slats for the front. From late summer into the fall, he sat outside for hours, whittling the boards to length.

Several barrack mates offered to help. Using pieces of glass, they scraped old glue from the joints of tables and bunks. Then Cline mixed the glue with a little hot water until it melted. After he'd glued the slats together, he shaped the contours of the instrument with his handmade chisel.

Cline felt he was doing something worthwhile—and it seemed as though every stroke of tool against wood brought him closer to home.

As the days grew short, snow and cold forced Cline indoors. He sat on his bunk, shaping the emerging violin in the dim light from the single window and one overhead bulb. He carved pegs to hold the strings, and holes in the neck to hold the pegs.

Next he cut elegant, f-shaped sound holes, sanded the wood smooth and applied a varnish. The other POWs watched in amazement. "Geez, you did it," remarked one prisoner. "That's a real violin!"

Not quite, Cline thought. Finally he obtained the strings and a bow by trading more cigarettes. By late November it was done. *I have music again,* he thought.

For a time everything he practiced was out of tune. He adjusted the placement of his fingers until he could summon a melody. Meanwhile, the men in room 6 decided to hold a Christmas celebration, and so Cline brushed up on some carols.

Then they learned of the German assault that breached Allied lines at the Battle of the Bulge in Belgium. The prisoners cursed the miserable weather that prevented the Air Force from aiding GIs on the ground.

The German commandant clamped down on the POWs, but they were still able to go ahead with their preparations for Christmas. One group planned dishes to be made from squirreled-away Red Cross packages. Another group made formal menus.

On Christmas Eve, Cline pitched in wherever he was needed, wondering what Anne was doing to celebrate the holiday. When everything was ready, the men filled their plates and ate.

At dusk the guards locked the prisoners in. Soon the lights were turned out. The men lit homemade candles. Some talked of the day's news about the Battle of the Bulge: the weather had cleared, letting the Air Force aid besieged GIs.

Cline reached under his bunk and pulled out the violin. Softly he began to play a carol. A few men hummed along, then started singing.

Cline imagined he could hear Anne's melodic voice over the motley chorus. He closed his eyes at the thought, finishing the tune by feel and letting the final note linger. Outside, the dogs patrolling the compound barked, and a guard uttered a sharp command. The room grew quiet.

On this night that symbolized everything that war was not, Cline once again placed his bow on the strings. Tenderly, with a slight vibration of the wrist, he drew forth the opening notes of "Silent Night." In resonant tones belying its humble origins, the violin spirited the men home to the peace and love they hoped would soon be theirs.

The men extinguished the candles and lay in their bunks, thinking their own thoughts. Cline stared at the bunk slats above him. Such simple wood had made an unforgettable Christmas. He fell asleep and dreamed of home.

On April 30, 1945, the Germans fled Stalag Luft I, leaving the Allied prisoners free to go. Nearly two months later Cline stepped off a train and saw Anne coming through the crowd toward him. After they hugged each other, Anne noticed the strange case made of aluminum coffee cans that he was carrying and wondered what it was. Today, over 50 years later, the violin sits in a display case on the Clines' living-room wall in Tacoma.

A DOCTOR'S PRAYER

BY

WILLIAM F. HAYNES, JR., M.D.

Alarm bells went off in my mind as I examined Anna, 60, in my office. Her usually cheerful face betrayed her anguish, and her dry, hacking cough told me she was clearly in trouble. Her face, lips and fingernails had a bluish cast, and she was breathing with great difficulty.

"How long have you had the cough?" I asked. Her eyes reflected her pain. "Three weeks," she replied.

"We're going to put you in the hospital, Anna," I said. "You've struggled enough." She nodded wearily.

We both knew what was being left unsaid. About eight years before, Anna had undergone hip-replacement surgery in a distant city, before routine blood screening for AIDS. Since then, she had enjoyed vigorous good health. There had been no reason to suspect that she had received contaminated blood in that operation. Until now.

I pushed her wheelchair the hundred yards or so from my office to the Medical Center at Princeton. Anna seemed too ill to be frightened, but I began to wonder if we were already too late. In the emergency room, Anna's obvious distress mobilized everyone to a rapid response.

"Doctor," she whispered as nurses established I.V. lines, "please—no throat tubes."

"All right," I replied. But I was concerned that one of the best means to ease her breathing had thus been ruled out. As we checked her arterial blood, I noticed how exceptionally dark it was, evidence that her lungs were not drawing in enough oxygen to sustain her. Within minutes, the lab report showed that a raging pneumonia was threatening to overwhelm Anna's body. We moved her up to the Intensive Care Unit.

The next morning tests confirmed that her pneumonia was AIDS-related. In spite of antibiotics, her vital signs continued to worsen.

As I leaned close to her ear to tell her exactly what we had found, she said again with great effort that she wanted no "extreme measures." I squeezed her hand to let her know I would respect her wishes.

I could understand her aversion to the ventilator. The strong, pulsing blasts of oxygen mechanically pushed into the lungs make breathing "effortless." But the machine can cause discomfort and claustrophobia; crowded by the breathing tube, she would be unable to speak.

"What if we try an oxygen mask?" I asked. She nodded slightly. But she was beginning to lose consciousness.

As we strapped the mask on Anna's face, she began to thrash about.

Now I was in a quandary. The more she struggled, the more oxygen she used up and the more her condition deteriorated. Sedation would calm her, but it would depress her respiration further. How could we keep her alive?

The level of oxygen in Anna's blood was decreasing dramatically. The arterial blood that should have been cherry-red was already nearly purple. But she was like a wild animal drowning. If she continued struggling, she would die before the antibiotic could take effect. As we tried to restrain her from tearing the mask off, defeat stared us in the face.

The only thing we can do now is pray. It was the kind of thing people think at such moments, and they often mean hope is lost. I looked at the two aides helping me. The respiratory therapist I had seen on many occasions over the years, and couldn't help noticing that she was a gentle, loving woman. The ICU nurse's name tag had a dove attached to it. A resolution formed in my mind.

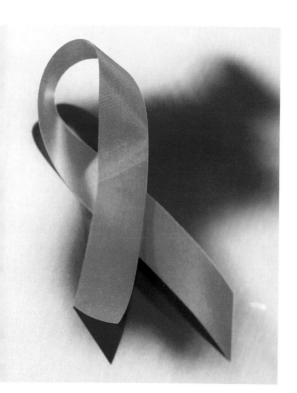

The nurse and the therapist moved closer, somehow sensing my intent. I leaned down to ask Anna if she would allow us to pray for her. Her head barely nodded.

Following my lead, the two aides gently placed their hands on Anna's head. "Dear Lord," I said, "give Anna peace. Let her know that she is in the palm of your hand."

We remained for some moments like that, Anna poised on the verge of respiratory failure—and death. I continued to pray inwardly, coming to the spiritual place I had first made familiar during my painful divorce. It was a place, I learned, of great solace and healing.

As we watched and waited, Anna appeared calmer, ceasing to struggle. During the next several hours she remained quiet, and small signs gave us further grounds for hope. Anna's blood gases began to improve, as did her color.

Within a few days, her fever lifted. She was taken off oxygen and moved to a regular room. Her appetite and strength returned. She walked out of the hospital days later without any symptoms of the pneumonia that had nearly ended her life.

A month later, when Anna came in for an examination, her stride was firm, her eyes were clear and her skin had a healthy glow. I took her to the ICU to visit the nurse and therapist, who greeted her warmly.

Anna was not by nature a demonstrative woman, but she hugged them, the depth of her gratitude and affection obvious. It was a quiet scene; no words were needed.

I never learned the nature of Anna's personal faith, if any. All I know is that her crisis confirmed my determination to call upon the power of prayer.

Many doubt such power. I know otherwise. In the lives of my patients and in my own life, I have seen the darkness disappear, the light come back. There is inner peace; miracles can happen; healings do occur; prayers are heard.

LITTLE DOG LOST

BY

DONNA CHANEY

Through the living-room window I watched our 15-year-old son, Jay, trudge down the walk toward school. I was afraid that he might again head out into the snow-blanketed fields to hunt for his missing beagle, Cricket. But he didn't. He turned, waved, and then walked on, shoulders sagging.

Ten days had passed since that Sunday morning when Cricket did not return from his usual romp in the fields. Jay had spent that afternoon searching the countryside for his dog. At times during those first anxious days, one or another of us would rush to the door thinking we'd heard a whimper.

By now my husband, Bill, and I were sure Cricket had been taken by a hunter or struck by a car. But Jay refused to give up. The previous evening, as I stepped outside to fill our bird feeder, I heard my son's plaintive calls drifting over the fields near us. At last, he came in, tears in his blue eyes, and said, "I know you think I'm silly, Mom, but I've been asking God about Cricket and I keep getting the feeling that Cricket's out there somewhere."

Although we all attended church regularly, Bill and I often wondered where Jay got his strong faith. Perhaps the blow of losing a much-loved older brother in an auto accident when Jay was six turned him to the Lord for help.

I wanted to hold Jay close and tell him that he could easily get another dog. But I remembered too well the day four years before when we brought him his wriggling black-white-and-brown puppy. The two of them soon became inseparable and, although Cricket was supposed to sleep in the garage, it wasn't long before I'd find him peacefully snuggled on the foot of Jay's bed.

However, that night I did tell Jay that I felt there was such a thing as carrying hope too far. Temperatures were very low, and I felt sure no lost animal could have survived.

"Mom," he said, "I know it seems impossible. But Jesus said that a sparrow doesn't fall without God knowing it. That must be true of dogs, too, don't you think?"

What could I do but hug him?

The next day, after sending him off to school, I drove to my real-estate office, where I forgot all about missing dogs in the hustle of typing up listings.

At two o'clock, the telephone rang. It was Jay. "They let us out early, Mom—a teacher's meeting. I thought I'd hunt for Cricket."

My heart twisted. "Jay," I said, trying to soften the irritation in my voice, "*please* don't put yourself through that anymore. The radio here says it's below freezing, and you know there's no chance of—"

"But Mom," he pleaded, "I have this feeling. I've got to try."

"All right," I conceded.

After our phone call, he took off through the field where he and Cricket used to go. He walked about a half-mile east and then heard some dogs barking in the distance. They sounded like penned-up

beagles. So he headed in that direction. But then, for a reason he couldn't determine, he found himself walking *away* from the barking.

Soon Jay came to some railroad tracks. He heard a train coming and stopped to watch it roar by. Wondering if the tracks would be hot after a train went over them, he climbed up the embankment and felt them. They were as cold as ice.

Now, he didn't know what to do. He pitched a few rocks and finally decided to walk back down the tracks toward where he had heard the dogs barking earlier. As he stepped down the ties, the wind gusted and some hunters' shotguns echoed in the distance.

Then everything became quiet. Something made Jay stop dead still and listen. From a tangled fence row nearby came a faint whimper.

Jay tumbled down the embankment, his heart pounding. At the fence row he pushed some growth apart to find a pitifully weak Cricket, dangling by his left hind foot, caught in the rusty strands of the old fence. His front paws barely touched the ground. The snow around him was eaten away. It had saved him from dying of thirst. Although his left hind paw would later require surgery, Cricket would survive.

My son carried him home and phoned me ecstatically. Stunned, I rushed to the house. There in the kitchen was a very thin Cricket lapping food from his dish with a deliriously happy 15-year-old kneeling next to him.

Finishing, Cricket looked up at Jay. In the little dog's adoring eyes I saw the innocent faith that had sustained him through those arduous days, the trust that his master would come.

I looked at my son who, despite all logic, went out with that same innocent faith and, with heart and soul open to his Master, was guided to Cricket's side.

Certain thoughts are prayers. There are

moments when, whatever be the attitude of

the body, the soul is on its knees.

VICTOR HUGO

"NOT IN OUR TOWN!"

BY

EDWIN DOBB

As Tammie Schnitzer came to a stop at the intersection near the synagogue in Billings, Montana, she noticed something on the stop sign. She got out of her car to take a closer look, and a shiver shot down her spine. A sticker showed a swastika over a Star of David and the words "Want more oil? Nuke Israel."

Suddenly Tammie recalled a conversation with her husband, Brian, when they began dating years earlier. "There's something I have to tell you," he said gravely. "I'm Jewish." Tammie was amused that he would make such a fuss over a difference that could never impede their relationship. Before marrying Brian, a physician who had come to Montana to work with the Indian Health Service, Tammie, a Billings native, converted to Judaism. Now on that morning in May 1992 she saw how life as a Jew could be very unpleasant.

The display of raw hate unnerved Tammie. She felt vulnerable and worried about their three-year-old son, Isaac, and eight-month-old daughter, Rachel. Then the 33-year-old homemaker came up with an idea. She called Wayne Schile, publisher of the Billings *Gazette*, to talk about the problem of hate groups in their community. "What problem?" Schile replied.

A few days later Tammie visited Schile. "This problem," she said, handing over hate literature which had been circulated in Billings.

Schile was stunned.

In the months that followed, Tammie returned often to Schile's office with the latest hate literature. Finally, in October, the *Gazette* ran a front-page story on local skinheads, detailing their attitudes toward minorities and their links to the Ku Klux Klan.

For most of the 85,000 residents of Billings, the story was a revelation of organized hate in their midst. But Wayne Inman, chief of the Billings Police Department, knew through informants that a group of angry young men and their hangers-on, most of them poorly educated and underemployed, were followers of the KKK, and he worried about what might come next.

On January 18, 1993, leaflets were placed on cars during an interfaith Martin Luther King Day observance at the First United Methodist Church. The fliers insulted a number of minorities, including the town's small community of about 120 Jews.

Inman called a press conference. "I can't do anything about this filth," he said, "because no crime has been committed. But the community can, and should, before it's too late."

Then Inman told a story. Before coming to Billings, he had been the assistant police chief in Portland, Oregon, where seemingly harmless leafleting had escalated to vicious crimes: minorities were assaulted, their property was vandalized. Finally, in the fall of 1988, three skinheads beat an Ethiopian man to death with baseball bats. "Only then," Inman said, "did the people of Portland acknowledge the problem."

"Silence is acceptance," Inman continued. "These people are testing us. And if we do nothing, there's going to be more trouble. Billings should stand up and say, 'Harass one of us and you harass us all.' "

In response, leafleting increased. Then one September morning, Brian Schnitzer drove to the Jewish cemetery to help pick up litter. Unlocking the gate, Brian discovered that most of the headstones were tilted or lay face down. Someone had vandalized the small burial ground.

"This is not a teenage prank," Inman later told reporters. "This is a hate crime, pure and simple, directed at Jews."

Meanwhile the leafleting attacks became personal. Uri Barnea, the music director of the Billings Symphony, who had emigrated from Israel, was singled out by name in fliers. On November 27, a bottle was hurled through his glass-paneled front door.

On the evening of December 2, a stranger stole into the Schnitzers' yard after Brian and Tammie had each driven away to attend meetings. Looking in a window of a well-lit room, the stranger could not have failed to notice Isaac's toys and the child-size bed. Nor could there have been doubt about the Schnitzers' religion. Resting on the chest of drawers was a menorah, the candelabrum Jews display during Hanukkah, the eight-day Festival of Lights. The banner on the window proclaimed "Happy Hanukkah."

The intruder heaved a cinder block through the window. Glass exploded as the concrete bounced across the bed and landed on the floor. Luckily, Isaac was in the rec room playing with Rachel and their sitter.

When Tammie returned, Brian led her into Isaac's room. Her legs went weak and she began to cry. Recalling the vandalism of storefronts that preceded the roundup of Jews in Germany in 1938, Tammie wondered, *Is this another Kristallnacht, the night of the broken glass?* "I'm scared,

Brian," Tammie said. "Whoever did this waited until we left. They were watching us."

They discussed restricting the children's activities. But gradually Tammie's worry turned to anger. *Why should my children have to live in fear?* Only one force could protect Isaac and Rachel, she realized—the community. Would anyone care enough to help them?

The next day Tammie called Schile. "You're setting yourself up for more trouble," Schile warned.

"I don't care," Tammie said. "This is a quality of life issue, not a Jewish issue." That evening, the Schnitzers observed the beginning of the Sabbath. They huddled in a corner of the kitchen, far from windows, and lit the ceremonial candles.

The following morning, Margie MacDonald sat reading about the Schnitzers in the *Gazette*. As executive director of the Montana Association of Churches, she worked to educate religious leaders about the dangers of allowing bigotry to go unchallenged.

One passage caught MacDonald's eye. The night of the attack, a police officer had suggested that Brian and Tammie take down their Hanukkah decorations. "How do I explain that to my children?" Tammie had asked. "I shouldn't have to do that."

MacDonald envisioned the people of Billings shielding the Schnitzers and every other victim of religious intolerance. Then she remembered the story of King Christian of Denmark. When the Nazis informed him that all Jews would be forced to display the yellow Star of David on their coats, the king responded that he would be first to wear it, and all Danes would follow his lead. The Nazis withdrew the order.

Now MacDonald reasoned, *What if, instead of the Jews removing menorahs from their windows, Christians placed menorahs in theirs?* She contacted the Reverend Keith Torney, pastor of the First Congregational Church. "Margie, that's a great idea," he said.

That Saturday afternoon, Torney called the pastors of several other churches, asking if they would distribute paper menorahs. The response was enthusiastic. Pastors reproduced the candelabrum and encouraged congregants to display it in their homes.

Torney gave out 300 paper menorahs at his church. And in his sermon that Sunday he said: "We dare not remain silent as our Jewish sisters and brothers are threatened. I will put a menorah in my window and in my heart, for what happens to Jews also happens to me. You must decide what your response will be."

On Wednesday, December 8, the Billings *Gazette* ran an editorial under the headline "Show the Vandals That Hatred Has No Place in This Season of Love and Light," urging readers to place menorahs in their windows.

A 68-year-old member of Torney's congregation decided to place a menorah on a window where it would be seen clearly from the street. As she taped it to the glass, a neighbor begged her to take it down. "Don't you know what's going on?" the neighbor said.

"Yes," the woman replied. "That's exactly why I'm putting it up."

Rick Smith, manager of Universal Athletics, placed a message on the reader board outside his store: "Not in our town! No hate, no violence. Peace on earth." Ron Nistler, principal of Billings Central Catholic High School, proclaimed on the school's electronic sign: "Happy Hanukkah to our Jewish friends."

A person consists of his faith. Whatever is his faith, even so is he.

HINDU PROVERB

Reaction among Jews to the sudden outpouring of support was mixed. Many feared the Schnitzers' efforts to draw attention to anti-Semitism in Billings would only further incite bigots. Thus, it was a divided congregation that greeted Samuel Cohon, Beth Aaron Synagogue's new student rabbi. The rift dividing his community preoccupied Cohon as he planned a vigil to precede Sabbath services on December 10, the third night of Hanukkah.

At 6:30 p.m. on that chilly Friday, about 200 people, mostly Christians, gathered across the street from the synagogue. As candles were distributed and lit, a small constellation of flames took shape around a pickup truck on which Rabbi Cohon and the Schnitzers stood. Cohon lit a menorah and blessed it, saying that it symbolized the human spirit. "You cannot stifle it."

Then Tammie stepped forward to speak. She said that the block that smashed her son's window was aimed at everyone who is a victim of prejudice. Just then a few skinheads arrived, glowering at the crowd. Staring at one of the young men, Tammie declared, "Leave our babies alone!"

Rabbi Cohon quoted British statesman Edmund Burke's observation on apathy: "The only thing necessary for the triumph of evil is for good men to do nothing." Then he led his congregants into the synagogue. The skinheads wandered off. But just in case, a few good people stayed to keep watch during the service.

The next morning's *Gazette* featured a front-page story about the vigil, a full-page color reproduction of a menorah and a statement urging readers to display it.

But the following day the paper carried unsettling news: small-caliber bullets had shattered windows at Central Catholic High School, near the sign that extended holiday greetings to Jews. The incident was a first in a week-long spree of hate crimes.

Late Sunday night, two families received anonymous phone calls: "Go look at your car, Jew lover." The homeowners found their cars' roofs stomped on and windshields shattered. Four other residents discovered their cars similarly damaged. None of the victims was Jewish, but all had exhibited paper menorahs.

Two nights later, vandals broke three windows that displayed menorahs at First United Methodist. The same evening, the glass doors at the Evangelical United Methodist Church were shattered.

"The hate groups are trying to silence us through scare tactics," Chief Inman declared. "We can't allow it. For every act of vandalism, I hope 100 people will put menorahs in their windows. It's impossible for a small group of bigots to intimidate thousands of citizens who stand together."

Tammie Schnitzer reinforced his remarks: "This is not a Jewish issue. It's a human issue." Then two local businesses announced they would distribute menorahs at all of their outlets in the area.

This time the entire town was aroused. Soon the nine-candle symbol could be seen everywhere—on office windows, in homes and apartments, on cars and trucks, in restaurants and stores, schools and other public buildings—thousands in all.

One night just before Christmas, Tammie Schnitzer took Isaac and Rachel for a drive around Billings. She wanted them to see that they lived in a community that stood by its children. Tammie pointed out the menorahs that hung in windows ringed by bright colored lights.

"Gosh," Isaac said, "are all these people Jewish?"

"No, Isaac," Tammie replied, "they're your friends."

Faith is like the little night-light that burns

in a sickroom; as long as it is there, the

obscurity is not complete, we turn toward

it and await the daylight.

ABBE HUVELIN

CHAIN OF LIFE

BY

PHILIP ZALESKI

*W*hen I was a college student in the 1960s, I enjoyed nothing more than lolling away the hours, especially on Sunday mornings, on the high, sloping meadow that overlooked our football field. Every so often, gazing down at the campus, I would spy tiny figures in suits and dresses streaming in or out of the college chapel. *How quaint,* I thought. *And how glad I am to be done with all that. Everyone knows the spirit dwells in trees and stars, not inside four plastered walls.* Oh, I didn't really mind my religious upbringing, but no child of mine would ever slog his way through that rigmarole. No way.

Two decades later, on a cold November morning in a cavernous stone chamber in Cambridge, Massachusetts, I watched nervously as a white-clad stranger poured icy water over my infant son.

"I baptize you in the name of the Father, the Son and the Holy Spirit."

How strange it had come to this, I remarked to my wife, Carol, as we walked home from St. Paul's Church. I still felt a nostalgic tug for the unfettered spirituality of the '60s. Homespun faith—prayers in the parlor, grace before meals and a stubborn refusal to subscribe to any public church—was the only kind of religion that made sense to me 20 years ago.

And yet, here I was, nudging middle age, springing mental cartwheels of joy as my son was initiated into a 2000-year-old, *very* institutional faith. It might have been Judaism or Methodism or Islam—but in my case, it happened to be the Roman Catholic Church. But glancing at four happy grandparents, at so many friends, and sensing the calm warmth that suffused my chest, I knew Carol and I had made the correct decision.

Bookstores bulge with reports of people returning to synagogue or church—mostly sad stories of broken lives reknit by faith. Our tale is different. It has nothing to do with despair and everything to do with delight, with the abundant fruits that religious affiliation brings.

For the most part, our friends profess little interest in organized worship. But those who practice a faith almost always cite the same strong reason. Religion, they suggest, is a way of capturing and solidifying the intuition that life does have meaning and purpose, that underneath the flickering surface of events lies a benevolence so vast it casts all our pleasures and terrors—the great tangle of romance, family, sickness, death—into clearer perspective.

Religion helps us reorder our priorities; we toss out the tin, save the gold and, in so doing, reorder ourselves. As psychologist and philosopher William James said: "We and God have business with each other; and in opening ourselves to his influence, our deepest destiny is fulfilled."

As for why we turned to the institution I had so long ignored—the reason lies in the gut, in a bone-deep feeling that the best of the past be preserved.

Perhaps the impulse began ten years ago when Carol and I visited the island of Malta, home of my maternal ancestors. There, in the vil-

lage of Birkirkara, a local woman pointed out a crumbling church: "*There is where your mother was baptized, and her father and mother before her, and their fathers and mothers before them.*"

The image flashed before me of a great chain of life, my ancestors linked arm in arm through the centuries—and, with myself as pivot, stretching forward into the future.

Now two, John is too young to know anything about God or religion. When we take him to Mass, he rarely lasts for more than five minutes before the shifting starts, then the clamber across the pew, the mad race toward the altar, brown bear in tow, before we manage to catch him and whisk him out. Yet we bring him anyway, so that the peace and beauty of the ancient rituals can work in his soul, on a level deeper than rational understanding.

I remember squirming in the pew when I was a kid, desperate to escape. But later I was always glad I had gone. Perhaps it was the solemn alternation of silence, chant and song—so different from the clamor of the schoolroom or television. Whatever the reason, something stuck, something good, and I know that now.

Last summer, our family moved to a new town. Along with checking out day-care centers, playgrounds and baby-sitters, our move meant finding a new church. We had been very happy with St. Paul's and wondered whether any new place could match it.

Shortly after we arrived, I left Carol and John behind for a scouting expedition—heading across town to a church perched on a hilltop, its twin spires visible for miles.

As soon as I entered, I knew I was home. A white Gothic altar crowned the graceful interior of stained glass and flying buttresses. On the arched ceiling, painted stars glimmered in a turquoise sky. Babies and toddlers and little pigtailed beauties crammed the pews. *This is it*, I thought.

Dropping to my knees, I was struck by the realization that religion is the perfect way to give thanks for my life and the lives of those I love. When all the other reasons for religion evaporate, the need to bow before life's great mysteries will remain. I wasn't sure then, and I'm not sure now, whether my return to the church came for John's sake or for my own, but I know in my bones—and deeper than that—that all of us will benefit.

Through the dark and stormy night
Faith beholds a feeble light
Up the blackness streaking;
Knowing God's own time is best,
In a patient hope I rest
For the full day-breaking!

JOHN GREENLEAF WHITTIER

"PLEASE, GOD, DON'T TAKE TRAVIS!"

BY
SALLY JOHN,
AS TOLD TO WILLIAM DEERFIELD

In major-league baseball, someone with a problem tends to keep it to himself, and people leave him alone. When my husband, Tommy John, suffered a torn ligament in his pitching arm in 1974, that career-threatening injury frightened everyone and caused us gradually to withdraw from our friends, just as they withdrew from us.

I was no different. A year earlier, when a friend learned she had cancer, I had been afraid to see her. I seldom called. How sad that we allow adversities to separate us. Usually. An exception came on August 13, 1981, the day we confronted a parent's worst terror . . .

Tommy was on a road trip with the New York Yankees. So the children—Tami, 7, Little Tommy, 4, and Travis, 2½—and I accepted an invitation to vacation at the New Jersey seashore with our friends Chuck and Carol Schaefer. My sister, Judy, and her children were in a car behind us.

All the way down I kept warning the children to be careful. Travis had a gleam in his eye. He was full of mischief.

As we pulled into the driveway, I realized there was barely room for Judy's car. Not wanting her to unload in a busy street, I pulled closer to the house. This small courtesy was to have a critical bearing on the events that followed.

After a glorious afternoon on the beach, we returned to the house. The boys were playing quietly in one of the upstairs bedrooms. I was in the next room dressing for dinner. All at once Tami screamed, "Mommy! Mommy! Travis fell out the window!"

I tore down the stairs and found Travis unconscious on the concrete. *This hasn't happened!* my mind screamed. Instinctively, I picked him up, hugging him to me.

"No, Travis! No!" I cried. He was limp and not breathing. Blood trickled from one ear; his skin had turned blue. His head hung at a grotesque angle. I looked up. It was *three* floors! Then the realization hit me: *He's broken his neck!*

"My baby's dead!" I cried. Above me the screams of the children were mingling with my own.

I could see the underside of Travis's tongue through his parted lips. I tried reaching my finger in, but his jaw was locked. Laying him on the grass, I groped for a stick, anything to pry his mouth open. *The nail-polish bottle!* I had been holding it when Tami screamed. Forcing the rounded top into Travis's mouth, I reached in and unfolded his tongue. With a rattling gasp, Travis took a breath.

Then the police arrived and rushed Travis, Judy, Carol and me to Point Pleasant Hospital.

Later, Little Tommy told me that Travis had been seesawing on the windowsill, bouncing against the springy mesh of the screen. The screen gave way, and Little Tommy saw his brother's feet disappearing through the window. Travis struck the hood of my car, then bounced onto the driveway. Had he hit the concrete directly, he probably would have died instantly.

While Judy and Carol filled out the admittance forms, I telephoned Tommy in Detroit, where the Yankees were playing. After an eternity, he came on the line. How does a wife tell her husband his son may be dying? There is no easy way.

"Tommy, honey . . . Travis fell from a window. I . . . I think he's broken his neck . . . Tommy, get here quick, *please!*"

"Honey, I'll be there just as soon as I can," Tommy replied.

I stood with Carol and Judy and cried. A nurse put her arm around me and asked, "Would you like to go into the chapel?" Mutely, I nodded.

There I threw myself on the floor in a fit of grief and anger. I begged, "Please, God, don't take Travis!" I tried to say the words, "Our Father, who art in heaven . . . Thy Kingdom come, Thy will be done . . ." But in my heart, I pleaded, "No, Father! Not your will, but *mine!* Please let Travis live!"

They insisted on taking me to an office where I could lie down. But I couldn't rest. The head nurse came in and told me that, incredibly, Travis had suffered no broken bones. "But," she added, "we must have your signature permitting the doctors to perform a cranial exploratory. There may be hemorrhaging."

I couldn't believe it: *they were going to operate on Travis's brain!*

"I can't just sign my child's life away!" I said. "I . . . I have to call someone!"

"Mrs. John, there's no time. If you don't, your child may die."

I signed, and the waiting began. An hour-and-a-half later, the doctor came out and told us that Travis had made it through surgery, but that he was still unconscious. It was too early to tell if there was permanent brain damage.

At 1 a.m., Tommy finally arrived, fully expecting to hear that his son was dead. Together we stood by Travis's bed. "Hi, buddy," Tommy whispered, tears filling his eyes. "Mommy and Daddy are here. We love you."

Then Tommy and I held each other. It was so hard, seeing our son like that. His eyes were open but unseeing; his arms and legs were flailing reflexively.

Tommy met with the surgeons. They had done a wonderful job in this emergency, but the next step was to get the *best* treatment available. Tommy called a doctor friend, who recommended that we contact Doctor Fred Epstein, a pediatric neurosurgeon at the New York University Medical Center in Manhattan.

After a sleepless night, we called Doctor Epstein. He recommended that Travis be flown immediately to New York. The surgeons who had operated on Travis at Point Pleasant disagreed; they said he might not survive the flight. Tommy and I prayed, then followed our instinct.

When we arrived at the medical center at 10:30 a.m., Doctor Epstein and a team of doctors met us. After the examination Doctor Epstein said, "Travis is in critical condition, but we don't see any sign of irreversible brain damage." Tommy and I fell into each other's arms in joyous relief.

"Mrs. John," the doctor said, "the most important thing is that you got your son breathing again in those first minutes. If you hadn't done that, Travis would have died. Now he's got a fighting chance."

In spite of the encouraging words, things didn't go well. Within hours, Travis suffered a series of spasms. These were brought under control, but his condition deteriorated. In an attempt to relieve the pressure caused by the severe blow to Travis's brain, four small holes had been drilled into his head at Point Pleasant Hospital. Now Doctor Epstein ordered another one. Then a tube was inserted through the skull to the surface of the brain. Hooked up to an oscilloscope, it enabled the doctors to get an instant reading on brain pressure. Travis's medication was also increased, but he remained in a deep coma.

He who prays for his neighbors will be heard for himself.

TALMUD

Days and nights went by. We hovered by our son's bedside, waiting for some sign that he was waking up. There was none.

Tommy reluctantly returned to the Yankees. After long, frustrating hours at the hospital, he needed to release his tension on the field.

When he wasn't playing, Tommy was with me at Travis's bedside. We'd sit there—Tommy, Carol and I—gently stroking Travis's arms, hair, cheeks. "Travis, honey, wake up. We love you so much. Please, open your eyes!" We'd talk like that for hours, until we were punchy. Chuck and Carol Schaefer interrupted their own lives for weeks to be with us.

Tommy was marvelous. His kindness toward others helped him bear his own pain, whether he was running to get coffee for the distraught parents of another sick child or autographing pictures for youngsters in the pediatric unit.

As the days passed, we became more aware of the magnitude of the public's response. People we hadn't heard from in years—and others we didn't know at all—called and wrote to say they were praying for us. Thousands of letters arrived from all over the country.

On the 16th day after the accident, as I sat gazing at my silent son, he suddenly lifted his hand and rubbed his eye. It was the miracle we had been praying for! But Doctor Epstein quickly warned us that Travis might not move again for days, even months. Our son had other ideas. In a few days his eyes were open and seeing. But his throat was still too sore from the tubes for him to speak.

Finally, on the 22nd day, Travis's lips parted, and I leaned close to his face. I held my breath as he whispered his first precious sentiments: "I'm hungwy!" A few days later, though, as he sat playing listlessly on the floor, he stretched his arms toward me and said the words I had been longing to hear through dark days and nights: "I wuv you so much, Mommy!"

A year later, Travis was fully recovered and as mischievous as ever.

Terrible as the ordeal was, Tommy and I grew from it. Because of those thousands of letters and calls and prayers, Tommy and I now understand how much people need one another.

All of us must at some point face heartbreak or a life-and-death crisis; when this happens, as Tommy and I have learned, no one has to hug his grief to his heart or go it alone. Instead, we should reach out to those around us—to family, friends, even strangers. We all benefit when we share our sorrow and need, if only to say, "Pray for me."

And when it happens to someone else, don't hang back because you're unsure of how to act or what to say. Reach out; be willing to be vulnerable. There are reservoirs of strength and healing in the touch of a loving hand, a sympathetic glance.

In our affliction, thousands of people reached out to Tommy and me, and we reached back. While God was healing Travis, that reaching was healing us.

THE SECRET LIFE OF ARTHUR WOLD

BY

SUZANNE CHAZIN

Sid and Phoebe Wold sat stiffly as the psychiatrist spoke to them. "I know this is hard news to take," he said, glancing at the blond-haired, five-year-old boy who sat beside the anxious couple. "But your son Arthur is severely retarded. He understands very little of the world around him, and will likely need special care the rest of his life."

Sid, a gardener, and Phoebe, a housewife, quietly left the University of Washington office holding their little boy's hand. By the time they arrived at their Seattle home that chilly fall day in 1967, Phoebe was crying. "What will we do?" she asked her husband. "How will we cope?"

The youngest of their three children, Arthur loved to laugh and hardly ever cried. Except for the fact that he rarely spoke, he looked like a normal, happy boy. Now Phoebe felt devastated knowing he would never be able to share his thoughts and feelings with her, nor she with him. Indeed, he was as gentle and unaware as a lost lamb.

The doctor said he'd need special care. An institution eventually? She and Sid would never consider that. Perhaps Arthur could never fully understand or reciprocate his family's love, but was love really love if it

90

demanded something in return? In the afternoon stillness, Phoebe lifted her head and asked God to look out for her little boy and give her the strength to accept the despair that swept through her.

Determined to give him as normal a life as possible, the Wolds took Arthur to church every Sunday and enrolled him in a day school for the mentally retarded. There, teachers tried to teach him to read and use sign language. Sometimes Arthur would utter words or mimic signs, but they made no sense. He flipped through the pages of books just long enough to look at the pictures.

Little things caused his family frustration. Arthur's chore was to set the table. Frequently he would just stand in front of a chair, clutching the silverware and staring at the plate. Or on outings, he wouldn't budge from the car. In groups, people talked through him as though he wasn't there.

As years went by, Phoebe and the family learned to accept Arthur's limitations. Every now and then, however, he would surprise them. Once, in a store, he ran up to a young woman and, grinning, extended a hand to her. Phoebe hustled over and admonished him, "Arthur, you can't walk up to people you don't know and shake their hands."

"But Arthur does know me," the woman insisted. "I used to teach him."

One of the few times Arthur's words ever made sense was when his beloved Aunt Swannie was due for a visit. He would look out the living-room window and ask, "Swannie come?"

When Swannie died suddenly, Phoebe caught herself crying in front of Arthur, then 13. Wiping away her tears, Phoebe looked into his eyes and said slowly, "Swannie died." A momentary light came to Arthur's blue eyes. "Swannie died?" he asked.

Surprised, Phoebe searched Arthur's face for a connection, but it registered nothing. Yet Phoebe sensed Arthur understood her sadness, for never again did he ask, "Swannie come?"

Moments like these made Phoebe and Sid more determined than ever to give their son a full life. They took him to Disneyland. They bought him a bike. Once, when their daughter Vicky wanted to go swimming with a friend, Phoebe asked her to take Arthur along.

"Why do I have to bring him?" the teenager asked. "People will look at us. Besides, Arthur probably wouldn't care whether we took him or not."

"If being at the lake is fun for you, it might be fun for Arthur too," Phoebe said.

Many of Arthur's feelings and thoughts were a mystery. But the family did know one thing—Arthur loved music, especially his mother's piano playing. So the Wolds found a piano teacher for him, about a ten-minute drive from their house. After Vicky got her driver's license, she would occasionally pick him up after class.

One day Vicky arrived late and expected to see Arthur waiting outside. But he wasn't there. Frantically, she raced up and down the streets, looking for her brother. What if he were lost and terrified on some unfamiliar street, incapable of communicating with anyone?

Unable to find him, Vicky drove home to tell her parents, her heart racing with panic. She burst through the door, and moments later saw Arthur calmly sitting in the kitchen, drinking a glass of milk. Somehow he had found his way home—a complicated journey he had made before only by car. *How did he do it?* His family longed to know. But there was no way their question could penetrate the shadows that surrounded Arthur.

Arthur grew to a tall, lanky, dark-haired 18-year-old with clear blue eyes that seemed to take in everything and absorb nothing. To give him some independence, Sid and Phoebe found a group home for him, and several years later Arthur was provided employment at a sheltered workshop for the developmentally disabled. Arthur would sit at a long table with other workers, assembling electronic equipment. Staff members at the workshop were kind, but Arthur had little social interaction because nothing he said made sense. Even in a workshop full of mentally disabled people, Arthur was alone in his own world.

Often on weekends, Arthur would come home for a visit and would tag along on errands with his parents or sit watching television. But it was a sad, empty life, filled with endless hours of nothing to do. Sometimes, Arthur would show anger by refusing to move or pushing his parents away if they tried to coax him into doing something. Phoebe knew Arthur was unhappy, but she didn't know what to do.

Everyone, from doctors to teachers to counselors, had long ago given up on her son, saying he'd reached his maximum potential. Sitting at the kitchen table one day, she asked God to help her let go of her hopes and sorrows, and to let Arthur live in peace and joy.

When Arthur was in his late 20s, a young, energetic woman named Carole Lewis Crane became a personnel manager at his workshop. Crane sensed there was something behind Arthur's passive demeanor. Sometimes, during lunch breaks, he would move his body to the music on the radio. "Do you like to dance?" Crane would ask, taking Arthur by the hand. Soon he was moving around the floor with her, a huge grin cresting his face.

When you say a situation or a person is hopeless, you are slamming the door in the face of God.

REVEREND CHARLES L. ALLEN

Then one day in September 1991, shortly after the Wolds returned from a month-long vacation, Crane phoned Phoebe. "I need you to come here right away," she told the mother. That afternoon, Crane led the Wolds into a small room containing a computer and keyboard. "I have wonderful news. Your son is not retarded. He is intelligent. In fact, he can even read and write."

The words hit Phoebe like a blow. For 24 years, doctors and teachers had told them their son was retarded. How could this woman believe otherwise?

Sensing their disbelief, Crane said quickly, "Before you say anything, I want to show you something." The young woman dashed out of the room and returned with Arthur. She sat him in front of the computer, then took a seat to his right. Phoebe and Sid stood behind them.

Crane's fingers quickly tapped out a message on the keyboard. Up on the screen, in glowing green letters, came the question: "How are you feeling today?" Then Crane turned to Arthur's parents and said, "Watch Arthur's eyes."

The young woman grasped Arthur's right arm and, bracing it against hers, held it over the keyboard. Arthur's shoulders hunched, his head jerked forward and his brow furrowed. Phoebe watched Arthur's eyes as they scanned the keyboard. Slowly, his right forefinger reached for the "I." Next he pulled back, hit the space bar and then the "F" key.

Arthur's entire face seemed riveted to the keyboard. Letter after letter appeared on the screen, each one executed in the same arduous manner. Arthur's arm began to twitch from the force of his exertion, but still he kept tapping out letters. Finally, Phoebe looked up at the screen. There, glowing, were the sweetest words she had ever read—words pulled from 29 long years of silence: "I feel happy because now I can tell Mom I love her."

Gently, she squeezed her son's shoulder as tears rolled down her cheeks. Sid, too, was crying. For a long moment, both were too choked to say a word. They just smiled at Arthur, who gave them a wide, triumphant grin. Finally, Phoebe uttered, "How did you do this? How can Arthur write when he can't even speak?"

"I went to a workshop where a woman demonstrated the technique," Crane explained.

It's called "facilitated communication." Devised in Australia, it was popularized in this country in 1990. The same or similar methods, however, had previously been independently developed and practiced in the United States.

The still-controversial technique has helped some developmentally disabled people communicate.

"Arthur and I have been working together for a whole month," Crane said. "And you'd be surprised how much he knows."

That comment struck Phoebe most of all, because deep down, some part of her had always believed Arthur understood more than any of them realized. "I think he's been trying to tell us that for a long time," Phoebe said, patting her son's shoulder as he grinned at her. "How did he learn to read?" she asked.

"He told me you always had lots of books in the house," Crane answered. "And from his special-education classes and watching television, he thinks he just picked up the skill."

Only one thing could make this moment better, Phoebe thought. "Please teach me to type with Arthur," she said.

Smiling, Crane tapped out the request, and Arthur slowly typed a reply: "I want you to learn."

The next time they met, Crane began by explaining the procedure. "Facilitated communication generally requires some physical support," she said, picking up Arthur's right wrist and placing it into his mother's hand. "You need to support Arthur's arm, providing a constant, backward resistance to give him the control he needs to move toward the letters he wants to type."

Sitting between Arthur and Crane, Phoebe started typing questions to which he could answer yes or no: "Have you eaten lunch? Do you remember your grandparents who died when you were small? Do you know your nieces' and nephews' names?"

As they progressed to more involved questions, every answer took forever to type out. Often, Phoebe would forget to provide enough support for a constant resistance for Arthur to work against, and he would mistakenly hit keys that resulted in misspelled words. After half an hour, Phoebe was exhausted.

Within weeks, however, the Wolds were discovering new facets of their son. For one thing, they learned Arthur had a sense of humor. When Sid asked his son if he knew what Labor Day meant, Arthur answered, "It means you labor to have a weekend." Another time, when Phoebe apologized for not having her thoughts as well organized as he did, Arthur joked, "I should be more organized. I have more time to think."

Arthur also had a unique way of looking at things. One day Phoebe asked him whether he could understand her spoken words. Sometimes, he told her, but other times he could only hear her tone of voice.

"What tone of voice do you hear when I speak to you?" she asked.

"A healing tone," he answered. "A soft and loving voice like the voice of God."

Another time he described his mother's piano playing "like a kite flying. The wind whirls the kite in circles, just like the notes."

Phoebe also discovered that Arthur knew math and could name the capitals of most countries. When they played "hangman" on the computer, he dug up obscure words, like "bream," a way of cleaning a ship's hull. He once described bad poetry as "doggerel" and a heart attack as a "coronary." It seemed there was little Arthur didn't know about the world.

As Phoebe's facilitator skills improved, their conversations stretched for hours, with Arthur expressing all his thoughts and feelings. His mother was amazed at the compassionate, thoughtful young man Arthur had become—though sometimes he would confess to moments of annoyance, anger and despair.

At Christmas, the Wolds' church raised money to buy Arthur a laptop computer so he could communicate with his family anywhere. People began to look Arthur in the eye when they spoke to him. He radiated more confidence and self-control.

One evening, when mother and son were nearing the end of a typing session, Arthur moved his hand over to the power switch and turned the computer off. Everything they had spoken about—family reminiscences, dreams and desires—was gone, its only place of storage in their memories. Phoebe was annoyed and told Arthur so. Then suddenly it dawned on her. Everything she'd prayed for all these years had come true. Arthur would never again be locked in a prison of silence. Her little lamb was no longer lost. Her own years of grief were now hemmed by a newfound joy.

"Do you ever pray to God?" she asked him, switching the computer on again.

"Yes," he answered. "Sometimes I pray for you and Dad."

Phoebe stared at him in surprise. "It seems strange and wonderful," she typed, "that you keep us in your prayers after all these years of keeping you in ours. What prayers do you remember?"

She grasped his hand, and slowly, he spilled out the words onto the screen:

"The Lord is my shepherd
I shall not want
He maketh me to lie down in green pastures
He leadeth me beside still waters
He restoreth my soul."

Believe that life is worth living, and your belief will help create the fact.

WILLIAM JAMES

Phoebe squeezed his hand. If anyone had walked through that valley of shadows, it had been Arthur. Over the years both of them had been wandering through shadows, lost to each other. Arthur's prayer was a prayer of thanks for both of them. She put his hand down and said the words she'd been longing to tell him since the day he'd first sat at the computer and lifted them both into the light: "Yes, son," she said softly. "Indeed, He has restored both our souls."

When in prayer you clasp your hands,

God opens his.

GERMAN PROVERB

"I HAVE NOT FORGOTTEN"

BY

HILARY LEIDOLF LOHRMAN

Standing on the doorstep of a decaying apartment building one windy morning several winters ago, I considered how my adolescent career dreams of starched white caps, crisp uniforms and clean, efficient "Ben Casey" hospitals bore little resemblance to the reality of my work. I was a psychiatric-admissions nurse for a Kansas City, Missouri, mental-health program. Many of my patients fought heartbreaking battles against chronic mental illness, and some were left helpless by their struggles.

I counted on my faith to carry me through the rough times, but some days tested my faith to its breaking point. The sting of the wind on my cheeks that morning was a reminder of how hard the winds of life can blow.

Clutching my collar tight with one hand, I knocked on the big double door that had once been painted a cheerful blue but now was mostly chipped away to its dingy gray primer undercoat.

"Mrs. Cameron," I called, "are you there?" I took my glove off and rapped sharply. "Mrs. Cameron?"

Moments later I heard shuffling steps. Someone fumbled with the locks. The door yielded warily, and an eyeball dotted the sliver of an opening. "You the nurse?"

"Yes," I said. She opened the door just wide enough for me to squeeze into the hallway. A cartoon program blared from a television in one apartment, and the stale smell of bacon grease hung in the air along with a baby's insistent wail. I followed Mrs. Cameron silently through the dark passage to her apartment. She was a slender, stooped woman dressed in a faded housecoat. Her feet wobbled inside a pair of men's shoes, and she kept one hand on the wall as she went. The referral form noted her diagnosis—chronic schizophrenia—as well as a host of minor but debilitating physical ills expected in an 86-year-old woman. She had listed no family or emergency contact person to help her and had refused all attempts to get her into a nursing home.

Inside the sunless, dusty apartment, nearly every flat surface was overlaid with photographs, postcards, newspaper clippings and notepaper filled with tiny writing.

I glanced in the kitchen. The sink was piled high with greasy dishes.

Mrs. Cameron fixed her attention on the window, which was covered by a heavy drape. "Last night the gypsy came through there to steal my things," she announced, trembling. Her eyes darted between the window and me.

"Mrs. Cameron," I said gently, "you need to be where you'll feel safe. Let me call your doctor, and we'll tell him what is happening."

I saw wild suspicion blazing in the woman's eyes. Somehow I had to convince her that she needed help, more help than I could give her now in this environment. But already I felt a sense of futility overwhelming me.

"Are you hungry?" I asked. She nodded, and I went to the kitchen. A framed copy of the Lord's Prayer hung on the wall. Where is the Lord in this woman's life? I wondered, fighting bitterness. I looked around me

101

and thought: Thy will be done. Sometimes, Lord, I do not understand your will. Opening the refrigerator, I threw out sour milk and spoiled food. One egg lay in a bowl beside a loaf of stale white bread.

I found a can of Vienna sausages and a bit of instant coffee. While water heated in the enamel kettle, I browned the sausages and made toast, then scrambled the egg.

I glanced around the corner to check on Mrs. Cameron, who sat slumped against the couch cushions, muttering to herself and staring at the window. Lord, I demanded, tears beginning to fill my eyes, how could you forget her? How could you forget this poor old woman?

The kettle whistled, and I assembled the paltry breakfast and carried it to Mrs. Cameron. I gently patted her arm. "Eat now, then I'll help you get dressed. Maybe we'll call the doctor after all." She looked into my eyes, and I saw that hers had softened. I washed the skillet and the dishes, and wiped off the counters while Mrs. Cameron ate every bite. Then I arranged her readmission to the hospital.

When the cab pulled up, Mrs. Cameron held my arm until I settled her into the backseat. Then she leaned toward me. "Thank you," she said clearly. "Thank you." And as she squeezed my hand, I suddenly sensed, almost as if it were an audible voice, the answer to my earlier prayer. For an instant the answer shamed me, but then I was filled with awe, and with gratitude: I have not forgotten her. I sent you.

For the believer, there is no question;

for the nonbeliever, there is no answer.

ANONYMOUS

LITTLE BOY BLUE OF CHESTER, NEBRASKA

BY

HENRY HURT

Frigid winds howled across the Great Plains that Christmas Eve so many years ago. The deepening freeze quickened the hearts of well-bundled children as the people of Chester, Nebraska, joined Christians around the world to remember God's gift to mankind of His only son.

Around 10 a.m. Charles Kleveland set out for Hebron, a town ten miles to the north. He took a back road, hoping to spot one of Nebraska's prized ring-necked pheasants. Kleveland eased his truck along the unnamed roadway through vast fields quilted in frost, his eyes scanning the stubble of corn husks.

"A flash of blue caught my eye," Kleveland says. "I stopped and backed up." As his eyes grasped the form, his heart went cold as the winter wind. "It looked like a child. I couldn't see it clearly for the tall weeds, but I knew that whatever it was, it wasn't alive." Kleveland reached for his two-way radio and told his secretary to ask Thayer County Sheriff Gary Young to meet him.

About 20 minutes later, Sheriff Young and prosecuting attorney Dan Werner stood on the frozen roadway. With the wind-chill factor ranging to 40 degrees below zero, they looked at the figure lying in waist-high weeds under a dusting of snow. Sheriff Young approached the body. "The boy's eyes were closed, and he was dressed in a light-blue blanket sleeper," says Young. "His left hand was resting on his chest, like he was asleep. I kept hoping it was a doll. Then I saw the hairs on the back of his hand."

The child, about nine years old, was dead. There, at the edge of a field on this bitter Christmas Eve, the questions came immediately. *Is he ours? Who killed him? Are our people in danger?*

The Christmas season in Chester had arrived wrapped in tradition and familiarity. Children listened to the story of Christ's birth, keeping a corner of their minds reserved for the gifts they might receive. Their parents, too, tried to focus on the real meaning of Christmas, but the spirit seemed thin. Despite one of the best harvests in memory, farmers had gotten low prices for their crops. People worried about the future. Now Charles Kleveland's terrible discovery accentuated the anxiety.

Within minutes, the news—often whispered so as not to alarm the children—had reached neighboring towns and then beyond Nebraska to Iowa and Kansas as well as Missouri and Wyoming. During this season celebrating the birth of a child, an unknown boy was found abandoned, frozen and dead.

As the news spread, fresh details emerged. The men who found the body suspected that the boy had been strangled. How else could the black marks around his neck be explained? Even more chilling were reports that flesh had been ripped away from his face. During these first hours, people assumed that the boy was one of their own. They pulled their children closer. Some checked the locks on their doors, as well as the ammunition in their weapons.

By late afternoon Sheriff Young established that the little boy was not from a local family, a confusing blessing. As fear began to evaporate,

it was replaced by resentment and anger—in some cases a vengeful anger—feeding the belief that someone from the outside had come in to commit this atrocity. People like that did not live in Thayer County.

In the evening, church bells rang through the cold air, calling people to Christmas Eve services. Parents held their children lovingly and protectively. The old hymns were sung through tightened lips.

At the United Methodist Church, Chester's largest, Pastor Jean Samuelson struggled with the confusion facing her congregation. Here they were, celebrating the birth of Jesus Christ, only to have had left on their doorstep the body of a child, abandoned and cloaked in anonymity. Somehow, she said, God was speaking to them. She left them with a promise: "Somewhere in God's eternity, this, too, will have meaning."

But as families slipped out of the churches into the night, worldly questions remained: Why was the boy murdered? Who was he? What monster could do this?

Late that night, husbands and wives quietly wondered about a much deeper question: If God was really a part of every life in Chester, Nebraska—and most believed that He was—then what did He mean by this?

The boy, whom some had come to call Little Boy Blue, had found his final resting spot in the heart of America. Indeed, Chester is only 50 miles from the precise geographic center of the country. The body was discovered only a mile from Highway 81, which stretches from Mexico to Canada, bisecting the United States. Tens of thousands of trucks and cars stream north and south; any one of them could have borne the little boy.

Authorities were optimistic about a speedy resolution. The boy was anything but a waif. He was well developed and properly nourished. His bone development indicated he was around nine or ten years old. He weighed about 55 pounds and was about four feet, three inches tall. His teeth were in excellent condition—not a filling or a cavity. He had sandy hair and light freckles on his face. He was a *cared-for* child—a loved child. Surely, someone, somewhere, was desperately seeking him.

Police were confident that this was a homicide. As soon as the body could be matched with a name, the authorities figured, they could connect him with the people who had left him. Arrests would follow.

But the dark markings on the boy's neck turned out to be freeze burns. Small animals had gnawed away the flesh from his face. It seemed certain the boy was already dead when placed along the road. There was not a hint of trauma or abuse. Despite all the examinations, no cause of death could be determined.

Another puzzle was that the boy's body was so clean, as if it had been washed. His fingernails were clean and neatly clipped. The cuticles of each finger were pushed back. His hair was clean and carefully cut. The bottoms of his feet were free of dirt, suggesting he had been placed in the sleeper after his death, which pathologists calculated took place on December 22.

All I have seen teaches me to trust the Creator for all I have not seen.

RALPH WALDO EMERSON

As the time went by, more than a thousand leads were pursued, including fingerprint checks and comparisons with dental records of missing children. Every major national and international resource was used in trying to identify the boy. Not one solid clue emerged.

Coming piecemeal, these developments nourished a stunning mystery. The number of well-preserved bodies of children this age that are not identified is so small that experts are hard put to find a single similar case. It is equally astonishing for medical experts, under comparable circumstances, not to be able to determine a cause of death. The mystery of Little Boy Blue—his identity as well as the cause of his death—is stupefying in its uniqueness.

Out of all this arose a sad but sure feeling: since no one seems to have ever reported the boy missing, it must have been his loved ones who left him along the roadside. For many in Chester, anger gave way to confusion, which mellowed into compassion.

People had puzzled over why the body was so poorly hidden. Indeed, a nearby culvert would have concealed the body until the spring thaw, maybe forever. Perhaps this child, Little Boy Blue, had died of natural causes and had been left in order to be found.

Three months after Christmas, authorities abandoned hope of easily identifying Chester's little boy. The county prosecutor released the body for burial. During the investigation, people from all over the country sent in contributions to give the child a proper burial.

As things happened, his funeral coincided with the most powerful and mysterious of all Christian observances: Easter. By this time a feeling stirred that, somehow, it seemed appropriate to call the boy Matthew, which means "Gift of God."

Close to 450 people filled the United Methodist Church on March 22, 1986. Pastor Samuelson turned to the 25th chapter of Matthew. In that passage the Lord commends the righteous for having fed Him when He was hungry, given Him drink when He was thirsty, taken Him in when He was a stranger and clothed Him when He was naked. In this story, when the people respond that they do not recall having ever done these things, Jesus replies, "I assure you, insofar as you did it unto one of the least of these, you did it unto me."

Jean Samuelson told those gathered that even today Christ speaks to people through the hungry, the sick, the lonely, those who are thirsty and naked. "This little one was a stranger, not clothed for winter, sick. He haunted me. I asked in prayer, 'Lord, why do you keep speaking to me about this child? Why should I feel guilt?'

"The answer: 'He has been in your life in other forms, and you have not heard him or seen him because you were too busy trying to prove yourself worthy.' "

She then told the congregation: "Those who left the little boy were probably once just like him—little children who fell through the cracks of a society that had not yet heard fully Christ's message to a selfish world. They may have been fearful of the law. They may have been confused or ill themselves. God is not asking us to know their hearts. *God is asking us to examine our own.*

"The boy's death and burial connect the two most important days in the Christian calendar, and that would seem to be a special sign to us. It is time we died in our old life and became resurrected to a new life— a life big enough to include one more little brother or sister or friend who has no one to care."

Then Jean Samuelson recalled the night the little boy was left. "I know there were tears by that roadside," she said. "The boy was gently placed on the ground, his hand over his heart. It was as if someone had said, 'I am so sorry, little one. This is the best that I can do for you. Rest now, and go home to God.' "

Jean Samuelson addressed the issue of anger and hate that had been prevalent when the boy was first found. "Christ is saying to us, 'Heed your own heart. Listen to your own words. Watch your own actions. When they are healed, you will see others with new vision, new forgiveness. I call to you from the bed of a cancer patient, from a prison cell. I look at you from the eyes of a starving child. I whisper your name from the body of a small boy left by a country road in rural Nebraska.' "

Then she bowed her head and offered the first prayer taught to millions of Christian children:

Now I lay me down to sleep
I pray the Lord my soul to keep.
If I should die before I wake,
I pray the Lord my soul to take.
Amen.

Out of the silence that followed there rose the voices of children and grown-ups singing, with no accompaniment, a single verse of "Amazing Grace."

The coffin, donated by a company in Kansas, was taken to the Chester graveyard. The gravedigger refused payment. The vault had also been sent without charge from a company in Kansas. In a plot given by an ill and widowed pensioner, Little Boy Blue was laid to rest in the dark Nebraska soil. The grave was marked with a red granite monument, donated by a company in South Dakota and by the Chester community:

Little Boy
Abandoned
Found Near
Chester, Nebraska
December 24, 1985
✽✽✽

Whom We Have Called
"Matthew"
Which Means "Gift of God"

Through summer and winter, people have kept flowers on the grave. Children leave toys there. The graveyard is along Highway 81, and hundreds of people have pulled off to look at the marker. It is even possible that those who left the boy have been to visit the grave.

People still talk about the little boy, and most hope someday to know the truth about what happened to him. Money that flowed in from around the country has been donated to Hebron's Blue Valley Care Home, where a new room will be named in the boy's memory.

The child is never far from Jean Samuelson's mind. "Great love flowed toward this boy from all of us, and great power flowed back," she says. "It is a power that brings us an understanding about ourselves that is so rare it can only be a gift from God.

"People were moved to examine their hearts. They learned the folly of judging others and making unjustified assumptions. The Lord allowed this boy to come into our community so we could better see ourselves. He was given to us not to stimulate condemnation of others but to help us find meaning in our own lives."

On this Christmas Eve in Chester, bells will ring out through the winter night. Voices will rise in celebration of the birth of a child nearly 20 centuries ago. Prayers will sound for peace on earth and goodwill among men.

The people of this little town nestled in the very heart of America will also think of another child who came to them at Christmas. That child stirred the eternal lessons of Christ, making them come alive for thousands of people.

"Christmas is a time for hope, for love, for joy," says Jean Samuelson. "We pray that God's love will overcome the fear of those who left their tears by the roadside with that little boy. Should they come forward, they will find the most precious of God's gifts—inner peace, the peace that passes understanding, the peace of Christ."

A good prayer, though often used, is still fresh and fair in the eyes and ears of Heaven.

THOMAS FULLER

EVERY EVENING

BY

JOANNE KAUFMAN

I made several vows when I became a mother, most of which were broken with astonishing rapidity. I swore that my children would never watch videos (one of my son's first words was "rewind"), and that I'd never succumb to movie-tie-in paraphernalia ("so what'll it be today, Pocahontas or Cinderella underpants?").

But there is one promise I've kept: for as long as my children have been verbal, they've said a nightly prayer, one I recited as a child, and still do:

> In peace, O God, I shut my eyes
> In peace again I hope to rise
> While I take my nightly rest
> Be with those I love the best
> Guide me in thy holy way
> Make me better every day
> *Shema Yisrael Adonai Elohainu*
> *Adonai Echod*

Hear, O Israel, the Lord our
God, the Lord is One.

My son and daughter are generally faithful to the script. But they have, on occasion, taken a few liturgical liberties. A few weeks after she'd graduated from the simpler "God bless Mommy, God bless Daddy, God bless Matthew" to "In peace, O God, . . ." Karen triumphantly navigated the tricky Hebrew pronunciation, then offered a spin on the translation: "Hell-o Israel!" she said. "The Lord our God, the Lord is Two."

Matthew, meanwhile, has recently taken to singing his supplications to the tune of "Oh, What a Beautiful Mornin'," thanks to his kindergarten music instructor, who has been teaching selections from *Oklahoma!*

Blasphemous? I don't think so, though I might draw the line at "The Surrey With the Fringe on Top."

Often my children wage an unholy war to see who gets to turn down the light in preparation for the event, who gets to sit in my lap and who gets to pray first. Sometimes they recite in unison, sometimes in a round.

Yet they've never resisted the ritual. It may be because they enjoy this nightly spirituality or—far more likely—they see it as yet another handy-dandy way to stave off the inevitable: bed.

Certainly over the period that prayertime has been in play, it has become a progressively attenuated affair that includes a discussion of the kids' favorite and least happy events of the day. Thus, I learned that the high point of Karen's day was sitting next to Stephanie during snacktime. (I hadn't been aware of Stephanie's existence.) And that Matt's most distressing moment was when his best friend wouldn't share a toy.

Lately we've added another segment to the ritual. I began asking the kids if there was anything they wanted to ask of God. From Matt, who's

afraid of the dark: "I'd like to ask God to make the night a little shorter." From Karen, who's grown clingy: "I'd like to ask God to have Mommy not go out for dinner tonight because I miss her."

The simplicity of their requests and their utter innocence compel me to issue my own silent prayer: "Please, God, let me freeze this moment forever."

It is during prayertime that I feel unambivalently like "a good mother." My hope is that through our shared prayer, my children are not only forming a connection with God, but by reciting my childhood prayer—taught to me by my mother, who learned it from hers—they are also forging a link to the grandmother who died before they were born.

It has also given me another opportunity to figure out just where I stand with my own beliefs about a higher power. The very existence of my precious children has reaffirmed them as nothing else could.

I believe.

It is not well for a man to pray cream
and live skim milk.

HENRY WARD BEECHER

OUR TRIP
of a LIFETIME

BY

ROBERT A. CALCAGNI

It is supposed to be a party, a reunion of old friends, the 35th anniversary of the adventure that still binds us together. But there we stand, speechless—half a dozen paunchy guys in our 50s hanging over a slide projector in a suburban Ohio living room, staring spellbound at the slim, frisky reincarnations of our teenage selves.

Some of us haven't seen one another in years. But memory holds us close. And now, in August 1992, we are together again at my house.

The slides work their magic: the present fades away. We are on the road again, California-bound, loaded shoulder to shoulder in the Cadillac limousine under Father Witt's imperious eye. We are rolling west, over the Rockies and on to the Pacific Ocean.

Now, reliving it on this summer night, we silently marvel that the likes of us—laborers' sons from industrial Youngstown—could ever have made such a storybook trip. But sometimes a picture clicking by illuminates that long-ago time with such clarity that the room crackles in a crossfire of remembrance.

"Look! There's that place in Iowa where we got in so late Father Witt said to drop the sleeping bags right where we were . . ."

". . . and we woke up with cops standing over us because we were camped out in the town square!"

"I bet they never saw so many Italians."

Uproarious laughter, then silence again as the golden days march across the screen. There is Father Witt sitting in the Caddy reading his prayer book while, outside, Jimmy Barone is sneaking a smoke. Next we are celebrating Mass in Yellowstone National Park, souls of innocence. Then we are gawking at a miracle—the new Disneyland.

No one is ever more prominently front and center than 15-year-old, five-foot-nothing Stevie Sinko, all sass and self-assurance.

I wonder if in our time two greater con artists than Stevie and Father Witt have ever been pitted against each other. Father worked his wiles on behalf of the Lord, of course, while Stevie, the Huck Finn of Youngstown, was an untamed spirit who could talk a blind man out of his seeing-eye dog.

Once, when we stayed over at a Trappist monastery in Utah, Stevie was smitten with the tonsures worn by the brothers of that order—a shaven pate, circled by a fringe of hair. Stevie bet us all the cash we had, $8, that he would get one of the monks to cut his hair just that way. We regarded this as found money, considering his calamitous entry into the dining hall the day before.

We had arrived just as the brothers were sitting down to the evening meal, the kind of timing at which Father Witt excelled. We were already well-briefed on the austerity of the Trappist order—a life of prayer and manual labor, long periods of silence, no meat—and we tiptoed reverently through the dining hall while the brown-robed brothers, heads bowed, waited deferentially. We were really moved.

Not Stevie. When we reached our places, he took one look at the food on his plate and said in a voice that would shatter glass, "Oh, well, Friday's a lousy night at our house too."

Yet the next day he found a brother in the bakery, spun out a tale of pious aspiration to become a Trappist, and turned up for supper with as neat a monk's cut as a person would want to see. So there went our eight bucks.

We were Father Witt's altar boys, but the best of us was no angel. Angels were in short supply in Youngstown in the 1950s. Bookies, numbers runners, loan sharks—yes. Angels, no. It was a tough town. And a prosperous one. It was Eisenhower's America, boom time, and if you wanted to work in the steel mills you could have a regular job and decent pay any time.

Growing up, we patronized the local dives and pool halls. We knew plenty of people in the rackets, including some relatives. They ran numbers, going around picking up quarters and dollars like door-to-door insurance salesmen collecting premiums.

It was accepted. The rackets were as much a part of the city as the smoke spewing out of the mills. It wouldn't have taken much to send one of us toward that dead end. We all knew 12th-graders making $10 a day just for running a few "errands."

It was Father Witt who made up his mind that *his* boys weren't going that route. He hauled us off the streets, off the sandlots, and tried to put us on the straight and narrow. And because Father Witt never tackled a problem in half-measures, he made our salvation his personal mission—and this, more than anything, is what got us on out to California.

Father William Witt came from a pioneer Youngstown family, the sort that always went out and worked to uplift the city. After studying at Ohio State and a seminary in Cincinnati, he carried on in that tradition. When he became a priest, Father Witt spent a lot of time trying to fend off the temptations likely to ensnare teenage boys. He took us fishing. He let us drive his car. When Jimmy Barone's mother died and his father was working two jobs, Father went every morning for weeks to roll Jimmy out of bed and make sure he got to school.

And the hocus-pocus he spun getting us to be altar boys in the first place!

We all went to the Immaculate Conception Church, a mix of Irish and Italian families where Father was assistant to the parish priest. But none of the guys I hung out with went to the church school; our families couldn't afford it. Most of us went to East High. And the parish priest had a rule that no public-school kid could serve as an altar boy.

We shrugged it off. Football was important. Basketball was important. Serving Mass was what you did if they forced you to.

Enter the Reverend William J. Witt, age 27, newly ordained and ambitious to be sent off to some Third World outpost as a missionary. "The East Side of Youngstown is a mission," said the bishop tartly, and sent him to Immaculate Conception. He stayed nearly nine years and, to our everlasting good fortune, saw my cohorts and me into young manhood.

On one Sunday after Mass, Willy—as we took to calling him when he was out of earshot—pointed to John Lattanzio, Ron Guerrieri, George Bonamase and me and said, "You four, follow me." That day we had our first instruction in serving Mass. Soon we were taking our turn with his other altar boys at the four Sunday services, plus weddings and funerals. We did not want to be left out of the warm fraternal circle he was building up at church; anyway, if you did balk, he was not above having a word with your parents. There was just no fighting off this gangling young priest with the cropped haircut and the unassailable certainty that he knew what the good Lord wanted for you.

As for the parish priest, I don't think he was any more of a match for Willy's verbal footwork than we were. I can just hear the monologues: "Reverend Father, I've come to know these boys and, God protect them, unless the church takes a hand here I'm afraid they're headed straight for perdition, because, Father . . ."

And so on and so on until the older man finally threw up his hands and said, oh, for God's sake, all right.

Of course, Willy was laying it on a little. We weren't exactly teetering on the edge of hell. We all came from good solid homes. Luxuries may have been in short supply, but there was usually a sound second-hand car in the driveway, enough food on the table for any pals you brought home, and plenty of love to go around.

We lived in a neighborhood of neat little houses and corner stores; it could be rough, but it held no surprises. It was ours. It was full of families whose people came from the same sorts of Old World villages ours did, and who now had the same worries and values and daydreams. We were streetwise enough to know there were dangers out there, but nothing we couldn't handle.

No one worried that all our livelihoods and this whole intricate social and economic structure were dependent on the steel mills. What could ever happen to the steel mills?

The fact is we looked at our fathers and could see ourselves 20 years down the line, and it didn't seem such a bad deal. It was a decent, comfortable life—a steady job, a car, a family, maybe a beer or two with the guys after work, some TV. What else was there?

It was Father Witt who started refocusing this perception for us. Listen, he would say in different ways, your mothers and fathers are the best in this world. They have made you a home and kept you safe from harm, and they did it with not much education and with bitter hard work. But it's a different world now, and you have a chance to go further than your fathers could ever dream of going. Do you want to turn your back on that just so you can get a job and a loan and buy a new car the day you graduate from high school?

The answer, of course, was yes—and some of us weren't even sure we'd wait to graduate. But we didn't have the nerve to tell Father that, so he kept working on us. We became his charges, his mission. His goal was to elevate our vision so we could see the landscape beyond the steel mills.

In our book Father was in a class by himself. Other priests worried about our souls; Willy worried about *us*. Did a boy need an after-school job? Willy found him one, mowing some parishioners' lawns. Was another kid in danger of being cut from football because he was failing math? "Here, let me see that math book," Father said. And he tutored him for as long as it took to haul an F up to a C.

But he gave you nothing for nothing. He made clear his utter conviction that effort was the key to getting anywhere. "Listen," he told us, "if you're slow, you have two choices: work harder or achieve less. There's nothing in between."

We thought he was going to become the first American pope. As it happened, he became something even more important—to us. He became the pivot on which our lives would turn. Unable to help us aspire to a world we couldn't even conceive, he made up his mind to show it to us. And then, finally, we would be able to choose between the existence we assumed was our lot, and possibilities not yet imagined.

One January Sunday in 1957, after the last Mass, he took us out for a spaghetti dinner and asked how we would like to drive to California with him that summer. We were struck dumb, all of us. California? He might as well have asked if we wanted to get signed by the Cleveland Indians.

We all started talking at once. "Yeah! When do we start?" Father explained that the music teacher, Mr. Cesene, with whom he used to go fishing, had moved to Los Angeles and had invited him to visit.

That was enough for Willy. In no time he fixed it up with our parents and was collecting maps and plotting a route that would take us to as many churches, seminaries and parochial schools as could be persuaded to put us up for a night or two.

We were to be seven: John Lattanzio, Ron Guerrieri, George Bonamase and me, plus Jimmy Barone, Don Lavanty and Father Witt. That spring Father made sure we all had after-school jobs so we could start accumulating the $125 he calculated we'd each need for THE TRIP—by now capitalized in our hearts and running rampant through our minds.

We walked on air and talked of little else. One evening a week we'd meet in the study at church. How much money did we have so far? How was the itinerary shaping up—meaning what churches had agreed to Father's request to feed and shelter us en route?

We assumed we'd go in Willy's car, a 1951 Chrysler; we were all so skinny that we'd often squeezed seven into it before. But soon we were eight. "Jim Dempsey's coming with us," Father announced at one of our meetings, to something less than wild enthusiasm. We had nothing against Demps. We just didn't know him. He was a bit of a loner, went to the church school, and came from a different neighborhood.

"How come we need *him?*" someone muttered.

You always knew when Father was teed off; he would pull his lips tight over his teeth and not say anything until the moment of anger had passed. Which is what he did then. And said, "We don't need *him;* he needs *us.* He needs our friendship. And we're going to give it to him." Silence. "Aren't we?"

"Yes, Father," said the mutterer.

But now we were in a bind because we couldn't squeeze *eight* into the Chrysler. Father said not to worry; the Lord would provide.

We'd heard that before, but worried anyhow. What if the Lord had other things on his mind?

Apparently he didn't. When Father decided he needed a bigger car for the trip, someone took him to see Florence Miller, whose husband, Sam, had died and left her half of Youngstown. Father explained that he was taking a group of altar boys on a pilgrimage out west, that we would be retracing the path of the pioneers and celebrating Mass and saying our rosaries every day.

Impressed, Mrs. Miller made the mistake of asking how she could help. "Well," said Father, moving right into his breathtaking mode, "one of Sam's Cadillac limos would be perfect for a trip like this—the one with the jump seats, not the one with the bar."

The poor woman didn't stand a chance. She said she wouldn't dream of loaning out Sam's car for such a trip. It was too much responsibility. Father said who said anything about her loaning it? He had come prepared to buy it, and how much did she want? $125? He knew it was worth maybe $3000, but he wasn't finished with her. When she said, all right, $125, but weakly mentioned that the car hadn't been serviced since her husband died, Father said no problem, and took it to Barrett Cadillac and had them put it in shape for a cross-country trip. And had them send Mrs. Miller the bill.

What with Father going around hitting up all the Catholic businessmen in town for a contribution, news of THE TRIP soon got into the Youngstown *Vindicator*. The local TV station, WFMJ, talked it up and gave us a camera and enough slide film for us to shoot a roll a day and airmail it back to them for the eleven o'clock news.

And Mary Sinko came storming into the church office one night dragging her Stevie by the collar and proclaiming that she couldn't do anything with him, and neither could his father or any of his teachers, and so the church just *had* to. "Take him to California," she wept at Father Witt.

"I'm not goin' nowhere with those creeps," said Stevie.

Father, who went at a challenge the way a moth dives into flame, sent Mrs. Sinko home and took Stevie out for a hamburger. I don't know who conned whom that night, but somehow they struck a deal. Stevie Sinko, a kid two years my junior but already a legend—for finding his way into a nightclub through the back window because, as he was 13 at the time, they'd refused to let him in the front door; for driving his father's car, eyes dead level with the top of the dashboard, and telling the cops he'd seen the car start to roll and only jumped in to try and stop it, never mind that he was headed uphill at a good clip—this five-foot bundle of dynamite was going to California with us.

Then we became nine.

We woke on Monday, July 1, with soaring hearts. It was D-Day at last. We assembled at my place, and the huge black 1949 Cadillac was backed into my driveway so the canvas-covered trailer we'd borrowed from a neighbor could be loaded with our gear: nine sleeping bags, two tents, a couple of suitcases, one paper grocery sack each for clothes and personal belongings.

There's a picture of us taken that morning, all with crew cuts, some still holding the rosary beads Father had given each of us as a going-away present. You can see the welling expectation in our hearts. We waved good-bye to our families, and with Father Witt driving, rolled out to the Ohio Turnpike and turned west.

When he drove, Willy was always turning around to talk to someone in the back. He thought blowing the horn meant he could forget about signals or the rear-view mirror. So at the first gas stop we persuaded him to move over, while John got behind the wheel. Thereafter Willy usually sat in the backseat while the rest of us took turns driving, except for Stevie, who was only 14.

How we loved driving that car! It had an automatic transmission and a big V-8 engine that just begged to go, and for as long as you sat behind that wheel you felt like the king of the road.

We fought over whose turn it was to "ride the bench." The Caddy had two jump seats, and to accommodate all nine of us, Father had laid a wooden plank across them so we rode three, three and three. Needless 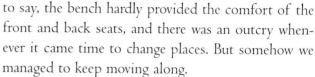 to say, the bench hardly provided the comfort of the front and back seats, and there was an outcry whenever it came time to change places. But somehow we managed to keep moving along.

Our first stop was South Bend, Indiana—Notre Dame. We wandered around the campus in awe of everything: the library that looked bigger than all of Youngstown University, the Knute Rockne memorial, the football stadium. In the dormitory where they put us up, we imagined legendary players of history's great Fighting Irish teams in our very rooms.

Next night we stayed at a seminary west of Chicago, arriving in time for supper—thanks to Father's acute sense of timing—stayed for a substantial breakfast, and did not decline the offer of sandwiches to take along for lunch. That became our *modus operandi*, unless the jump between school or seminary beds was too far; then we'd roll out our sleeping bags in a quiet spot off the road, and Father would grill hot dogs over a campfire.

If there was a Catholic church nearby, he'd knock on the door and go into his song and dance about how he was taking "these young pilgrims" on a journey of religious discovery, and was there somewhere nearby they could find a hot meal? Sometimes the best we could do was a cheap restaurant; more often the parish priest invited us home.

Father Witt could see that his audacity embarrassed us, and his response was classic Willy: "I know, the Bible says the meek shall inherit the earth. But do you know what else it says? That the just are bold as lions."

He made his philosophy crystal clear, that we were all here on earth to help one another. On this pilgrimage we were going far on limited funds, and people's offerings of food and shelter along the way were God's gifts. In our lifetimes, he predicted, we were going to repay these gifts manyfold.

Another time he put it more bluntly: "Don't be afraid to speak up for yourself. Nobody sees the invisible man."

It was a valuable lesson. Years later, whenever I needed a jolt to approach someone, I said it to myself, *Nobody sees the invisible man.*

Willy wasn't overstating the "religious discovery" part of the trip by much. We attended Mass every morning and said a rosary every night—and whenever the constant shoulder-rubbing of eight zesty teenagers erupted into mayhem. "Okay, calm down," he'd order. "Now, gentlemen, get out your beads, and we will offer up a prayer for brotherly love."

He made it a rule not to hear our confessions, but we stopped at enough churches that there was plenty of opportunity for other priests to hear them. We needed all the absolution we could get. We smoked behind his back; we told dirty jokes; and, boy, did we have impure thoughts! Stevie, always conjuring up new devilment, took to hanging back in restaurants and rifling our tips.

As if his real offenses weren't bad enough, Stevie also "confessed" to outrages he could barely pronounce, always leaving his confessional door open to us, his appreciative audience. More than once we heard an awestruck priest gasp, "You did *what?*"

One day he approached the dimly lit confessional waving a sheet of paper and declaiming, "You gotta get some light in here. You can't expect me to remember all this."

Before we left, Father said we older boys should set an example and help channel his terrific creativity in a useful direction. I took this to mean that I should lean on him when he got out of line, so I did. But since he was forever out of line, I was forever rapping him on the head. "Shape up, squirt," I'd say.

"Drop dead, big guy," he'd answer. He never called me Bob. It was big guy, or Cal.

Once at a truck stop, I got in the back with him, and he pulled this metallic object out from under his shirt, finger on the trigger, and said out of the corner of his mouth, "What do you think of this, big guy?"

"Stevie," I whispered. "That's a real gun."

"Damn right it is. Now go ahead and rap me on the head."

Then Willy opened the back door, saw the gun, looked Stevie in the eye and took it away from him without a word. A frantic trucker came running out of the restaurant yelling, "Hey, did anybody see the gun I left in the toilet?"

"Here it is, son," said Father quietly. "One of my young men was just going to turn it in."

The poor guy was so grateful he tried to give Father a $5 reward, but Father said no, thanks, and Ronnie said, "Gee, that's the first time I ever saw him turn down an offering."

We rolled on, discovering America, young Columbuses coming upon a new world every day. Davenport, Iowa City, Des Moines. Then the corn-covered plains of Iowa gave way to the great western prairie, a vast realm of grassland reaching to far horizons; Omaha, and beyond that the South Dakota Badlands, a fantasy of tawny buttes and spires and shadowed canyons sculpted by the winds of eons past, and by rivers long gone. Jim Dempsey, who usually spoke only when he had to go to the bathroom, put it for us all when he said, "I'm never going to forget this."

As we continued on, the Caddy became like one of us. We called it "she" and imbued her with characteristics we admired—"she" was hip; she had it (thumb on chest) *here*. Immaculately tended when we started out, she soon took on the look of all the miles we were rolling up: insect-spattered windshield, road grime dulling the gleaming finish. There was no air-conditioning, so we drove with the windows wide open, which was just as well, since we tended to leave sweaty socks and T-shirts lying around the seats.

One afternoon we stopped near a high hill. Father sent us off to climb it. It was hard work, but when we came up over the last crest and reached the top, we discovered another new world: the Rocky Mountains. To the west, seeming almost untouchable in the untarnished sky, there ranged a parade of soaring peaks that rendered insignificant anything we had ever seen. *We* felt insignificant, and yet uplifted, inspired. Suddenly I wanted to be better than I had ever been, to be worthy of these American wonders.

We knew from the first days that the trip was going to stay with us forever. We had been let out of a sealed box called Youngstown, and the first thing we learned was that Youngstown wasn't the world. Father was also teaching us a new self-reliance: "*You* can pick up your own dirty socks, just the way your mother did; you can even wash them." We assumed duties without being asked to: John Lattanzio kept the accounts of our expenditures; at each gas stop John and I checked the oil and tire pressure; George made up the driving schedule. And whenever Don Lavanty saw an untended hose, he shooed us all out of the car and washed her down.

Each of us, in his own way, tried to store up the memory. Willy became fanatical about taking pictures for WFMJ-TV, suddenly calling out, "Oh, say, pull over here—I have to get a shot of this." And then focusing and fooling with the f-stops until once Don Lavanty yelled, "Hey, Father, they painted Whistler's Mother faster than you're taking that picture." Meanwhile, I was clicking away with my Kodak Hawkeye, George was keeping a diary, John wrote long letters to his girlfriend, and everyone else sent postcards home.

We had plenty to write about. In South Dakota, one morning, after we'd had a cold church supper the night before and had to sleep on the vestry floor, Father allowed us to have a real breakfast in a real restaurant. We stopped at a place, but the manager said he couldn't seat nine people together—meaning not nine like us.

We were a scruffy lot that morning, uncombed, unwashed. "Of course you can," Willy declared, and he began moving customers and tables around as if he owned the place. Pretty soon we were seated and ordering up a storm of food.

Then some of us went to the men's room. On the wall was a condom-dispensing machine, something you didn't see around Catholic Youngstown, and there followed predictable remarks and gales of laughter.

In walks Willy. He zeroes in on the source of our revelry, and with lips drawn tight against his teeth, he slams the offending device with his fist. In his wrath he seizes the machine as if he is going to rip it off the wall.

At which precise moment a kitchen hand enters, takes in the scene and says, "What's the matter, Father? Your quarter stuck?"

I think only Willy's priestly roots saved that young man from grievous bodily harm. "Out!" he ordered us. "Out!"

We scooted through the door, no longer able to control our laughter as he stalked up to the others and commanded again, "Out!"

By now the food had arrived. All the guys, ravenous, poised over heaping plates and about to banish the memory of two days of cold, limp sandwiches, looked up, dumbfounded. "What?" they mumbled.

"Out, all of you, out! We'll not eat one morsel where they sponsor sin."

By this time the manager came running up, imploring, "What is it? What's the matter?" And while Father was unambiguously telling him—interspersing commands for us to get out, out, out—we crammed food into our mouths, stuffing toast into our pockets, scooping up bacon, sausages, containers of milk, rolls, butter, and fleeing finally, at his last, unappealable "OUT!"

Once we were back in the car and had laughed ourselves dry, we settled down and ate everything. We even lit up, knowing that Father was not about to let that manager off with a mere tongue-lashing. His anger would pass, and then the level of the transgression would call forth an expanded, soul-saving sermon.

We almost got caught at that. Willy came striding out before we could ditch our butts, and George, who was 18 and allowed to smoke but didn't, wound up holding five cigarettes.

Father never noticed. He was transcendent. "We'll have to say a prayer for that man," he said. "Down deep he's a good person."

Day by day, we advanced westward, pushing on. Cody. Shoshone National Forest. Father Witt never let us forget that we were traveling in the path of the early settlers. The very ground we were covering in a matter of days had taken them months in wagons drawn by oxen, hauling all their possessions across a hostile and uncharted wilderness. He admonished us to keep those brave souls close to our hearts because—in leaving their familiar worlds to go looking for a place in this unknown America where they could do better—our own parents and grandparents were pioneers too. Don't think that didn't make us sit up and listen.

The day we put up our tents on the shore of a lovely crystal lake in Yellowstone National Park, we stayed awake half the night, spellbound, while Father spun stories of the West. He told us how the look of the land, for hundreds of miles, was unchanged from the days when the settlers passed through. There were goose bumps all around when he said that more than one wagon train had undoubtedly pitched a camp where we now sat around the fire.

Long days on the road were a trial. We argued over who would drive and who would sit where. As it must also have been for the pioneers, much of the plodding on to the next destination was just plain monotony.

Only Jim Dempsey was endlessly entranced. He seemed thrilled just looking out the window. Demps was slight, with a high-pitched voice and big eyeglasses—we called him Mr. Peepers until Father saw his hurt and made us quit. I think this trip was the first time he'd ever been part of a social group. For all I know we may have been the first friends he ever had.

Stevie taught him to play poker, then cheated him shamelessly. "Whaddya got there, Demps? A straight? Ah, too bad. I got me a royal dude."

Whatever animated Stevie was his secret, but his brass was always on public display. As often as Father might talk about the Bible, Stevie came back with taunting questions: How come no one had ever seen God? Why should people believe in Him if He never showed up?

"People don't see electricity, either," Father replied reasonably. "But no one doubts it's there."

"Yeah, that's because if you mess with a live wire you get a hell of a shock," said Stevie.

"Yeah, and if you mess with God, you'll get the same thing," Willy said.

Willy, for whom God was right *here*, riding west with us, worked his wonders every day. "Hey, Father, we're just about running on empty," I said as we tooled along a sparsely settled stretch of Wyoming highway. "Shouldn't we take one of these side roads and find a gas station?"

"Oh, there'll be one up ahead soon," he answered. "Have faith."

I wanted to tell him I had plenty of faith, but the car ran on gas, of which there was now precious little. What I said was, "Gee, Father, we're in the middle of nowhere here. If we run dry—"

"The Lord will provide," he told me serenely.

It made me mad. It was as though the car didn't mean anything to him, whereas to me it had come to be more a person than a thing. It had never let us down.

Fifteen minutes later, still without a sign of life in any direction, the engine shuddered twice, surged and died. The Caddy rolled to a stop in eerie silence.

Willy remained unperturbed. He glanced out the window, then went back to his prayer book. "Father," I said, trying not to gloat, maybe not trying too hard, "in case you didn't notice, we just ran out of gas."

"I suggest you all get out and stretch your legs while we're waiting for help."

"What help?" I grumbled. "We haven't seen a car in either direction for an hour."

Whereupon a pickup truck came over the hill. A grizzled guy in a cowboy hat got out and asked if we had a problem. Within minutes he had emptied a five-gallon gas can into our tank, refused payment, accepted Father's blessing, and told us where to find a gas station. And we were once again on our way.

"Father?" I said meekly.

"No apologies necessary," he replied.

We pulled into Salt Lake City longing for a good spaghetti dinner, but it was nearly 9:00 p.m., and in Mormon Utah that was bedtime. When we finally found an open restaurant, we got a soggy mass of wildly overcooked something doused in ketchup. In revenge, Stevie pocketed not only the tip, but a pair of salt and pepper shakers he thought his mother might like.

This time Father caught him. He marched him back to return the pilfered items and returned to the car with his lips *very* tight against his teeth. Later, he took me aside and said, "You're not doing Steve any good, Bob, rapping him on the head when he makes you mad, but laughing when he takes things that don't belong to him."

He had touched a nerve. I knew what he said was true, and could only lamely reply, "I'm not the only one, Father."

"Of course not, and that's the trouble. He does these despicable things for one reason: to win *all* of you. And he doesn't mind taking a few raps on the head if you'll laugh the rest of the time."

I was still worrying that around in my mind when, the next evening, we set out across the Nevada desert. Even with all the windows open, the heat was suffocating. A broiling ball of setting sun glared in our eyes for hours, then dipped below the edge of earth and left us following our slender cone of headlight through a night so black the stars shone brighter than the marquee of the biggest movie house in Youngstown. Those who could, slept.

We stopped once for gas, then not again until daybreak when, hungry and dehydrated, we pulled up at a sagging one-pump gas station, still 100 miles short of California. We bought a gallon of water—nobody *gives* water in the desert.

Leaning against the car, we drank the warm water and took the sandwiches Father was making out of the food we had left in the trailer: cornflakes, mustard and some two-day-old bread.

We had to be grateful for this food, Willy said earnestly. It was *good* food, and hadn't he always told us the Lord would provide? After the sermon we said grace and ate the sandwiches. They weren't that bad.

In case anyone missed the lesson that we needed to be thankful for even the smallest gifts, Father nailed it down by telling about the tragic Donner party, in whose tracks we were now following. They had started out from Illinois in the spring of 1846, with plenty of cash to help them forge a new life in California. Their cows and oxen and sturdy wagons stretched out for miles across the desert trail. They were full of hope and courage.

But they did not have an experienced leader, and they were short on food and winter clothing. Most of all, they were short on luck. Exhausted by their long trek across the desert in the full heat of summer, they rested for a time by the sparkling Truckee River, where the city of Reno would rise. This delay was their undoing. By the time they started up into the Sierra Nevada, early snowstorms were upon them, and paralyzing winds. They pushed on, braver than they were wise, for when they reached the summit and could no longer turn back, 20-foot snowdrifts blocked the way ahead. They were snowbound in the High Sierra.

At that point Father stopped, and we all leaned toward him anxiously. Someone implored, "Yeah? Yeah? So then what happened?"

But the part of Willy that was pure showman had taken over. "The rest comes later," he said, and no matter how hard we begged, that was as far as he'd go.

On we rolled, to Virginia City, whose gold and silver mines once made it one of the richest towns in the West; and to Lake Tahoe, where we raised our tents on the beach. We could not get the Donner people out of our minds, imagining that they might have rested here too. Then we set off in early morning light, up into the mountains.

We sped through a wilderness of fir trees and towering rock, seeing images of the doomed pioneers struggling over trackless snow. Then, near the crest, close to a place now called Donner Pass, which a century later was still the main route into California, Father ordered the car stopped. And there, he told us the rest of the story.

Food ran low. The livestock wandered off. By December, four among the group were dead, and the strongest of the men and women set off on a desperate search for help. But soon they began to die off too. Those who lived endured unutterable hardship, but struggled on.

On January 10, 1847, five women and two men stumbled into an Indian village near the Sacramento Valley. Relief parties started for the pass, but it was April 22 before the last of the survivors—47 devastated souls—were brought down to safety. Their numbers had been 89 when they started west.

No one spoke as we got back into the car and crossed into California. I guess we were all imagining ourselves with those brave pioneers. Would we have had the courage to face their terrible trial? Could we be heir to their indomitable American spirit? Then I thought about our immigrant parents, and I decided yes, yes, we could.

San Francisco was another new world, and Father presented it with a flourish. Nothing among all the wonders we'd seen prepared us for Chinatown, a dazzling farrago of exotic faces, neon lights and mysterious shops. "Look! Look at that!" we kept calling giddily.

And the cable cars! Can you imagine a kid who'd only ridden Youngstown's staid trolleys plunging almost straight down Hyde Street to San Francisco Bay on a cable car?

Willy took us to Fisherman's Wharf, where we ate shrimp broiled in heaven, and to the water's edge. "This is the Pacific Ocean," he said, as if he was introducing us to a cardinal of the church. "It goes from here to Alaska, Japan and Australia. Stick a finger in and taste it so you'll remember—there isn't anything on this planet bigger than the Pacific Ocean."

After a few days of sightseeing came the bad news. Father announced he had to go north to visit a friend in a monastery. He seemed to wrestle with his conscience, but finally he said, "I feel I can do this because I believe in you."

We stared back like an octet of dummies, poised between elation and panic. We were to drive to Los Angeles and stay with the Cesene family, as planned, he said, and he would join us in three days. Here were the address and telephone number. Here was some money to see us through, and here were his blessings and God's wish that we be the responsible young men he knew we could be.

It all went so quickly. Suddenly we were parked under the airport "Departures" sign, and Father Witt was getting out of the car, actually leaving. He stuck his head back into the open window for a final message: "If you want to smoke yourselves into early graves, I can't stop you," he said. "But quit lying about it." He rummaged around in the trailer for his grocery bag of extra underwear, waved and was gone.

"Yippee," said someone in the back, so gloomily that it registered on the brain as, "Oh, no." But when you're a teenager, nothing is final or fatal. By the time we started tooling south on U.S. 1 we were exhilarated. We were on our own!

Pretty soon we were belting out "One Kiss Led to Another," replete with "shooby doos," while a couple of guys kept time by slapping their palms on the outside of the car door. We began to sound better and better.

What we looked like was something else. Around noon, we marched into a restaurant—black T-shirts, straw cowboy hats, Stevie in his partially grown-in monk's tonsure—and ordered 16 hamburgers, a pile of french fries, six beers, and a Coke for Demps and Stevie. Willy wouldn't have let us spend that much in a week.

We had the same for dinner and then rolled our sleeping bags out on the beach. It was glorious. Who needed Father Witt?

By the time we got to Los Angeles, we felt like kings of the road. But when I telephoned Mr. Cesene for directions to his house, he punctured our euphoria. Something had come up, he said. His relatives had arrived unexpectedly, and there was no room for us.

"But don't worry," he hastily added. "You could try the basement of the Blessed Sacrament Church on Sunset Boulevard."

I wrote down the address halfheartedly; none of us wanted to sleep in another church basement. So we sat in the parked car wondering what to do next, the blur of evening traffic and the dazzle of big-city lights unnerving us. Then old Demps cleared his throat, and we all turned his way because he never spoke unless it was important. "Um, I have relatives who live in L.A.," he said. "Maybe—"

"Yeah, yeah, call them!" we all agreed eagerly, and in seconds we'd rushed him into a phone booth and were holding the number up in front of his eyes while he dialed.

No answer.

We found another hamburger place, ate, called again. Still no answer. We sent George into a package store to buy beer because he was 18, and then decided to drive out to Dempsey's relatives' house and wait for them to come home.

We finally found our way to a modest bungalow in Whittier, a few miles from L.A. We pulled into the driveway and got out. The house was pitch-black. By now it was past 11 p.m., and the whole neighborhood was dark. We rang the doorbell. No one answered.

Somebody said what we were all thinking: "What do we do now?"

Stevie sidled up and, giving me his best side-of-the-mouth Humphrey Bogart, said, "Hey, big guy, you want to get inside this place? I been around back checking it out. I figure it'd take me five minutes. No broken glass."

"Oh, get lost, kid," I snarled.

Which was exactly the wrong thing to do. Not five, but three minutes later, the lights in the house went on, the front door opened and there stood Stevie, with a hyena grin and a sweep of his arm to usher us in. "Welcome to Dempsey's California pad."

"Wait a minute," I called at the headlong rush for the door. No one even looked back. I ran in and asked Demps, "Hey, what about this?" He shrugged his shrug that meant anything you guys want to do is okay with me. So I thought, *What the hell.* And I got into the spirit of the thing.

We started working on our beer, and pretty soon we were putting everything from the refrigerator on the kitchen table. John said he'd make an omelette, and started frying onions and beating eggs.

Every light in the house was blazing. The radio was blasting out rock 'n' roll. By then it must have been close to midnight, so we brought in the sleeping bags.

Boom! The front door is flung open and in busts some enormous guy, wearing a bathrobe and a red face. "What's going on here?" He has to yell to be heard above the radio. "What the hell do you think you're doing in this house?"

It's Stevie who speaks up, naturally. "We're *his* friends," he says, pointing to Demps.

"And who the hell is *he?*" The man is still yelling, although someone has turned off the radio. The rest of us stand there, frozen.

But Stevie goes toe-to-toe with him. "He's Jim Dempsey. His relatives live here." He pulls himself up to his full five feet and says, "And who're you, busting in like that?"

"Neighbor, idiot! You clowns woke up the whole neighborhood." He looks us over for a moment and starts for the door. "We're gonna see about this." His parting words shatter our ossified state: "I'm calling the cops."

The door hadn't even closed when, like a Keystone Kops comedy thrown into double time, we began snatching up shirts and shoes, stuffing sleeping bags back in the trailer, all the time bracing for sirens and flashing lights. I jumped into the driver's seat and struggled to back the Caddy and the trailer out of the driveway.

We wound this way and that looking for a place to sleep, and finally turned into a side road that looked just right because it was marked "No Trespassing." When we pulled off and cut the ignition, we heard this steady, whirring thump of a sound. We laid out our sleeping bags and collapsed. When we woke up in the morning, we found ourselves in the middle of an oil field. The whirring thumps were the endless throbs of the pumps.

We had rolled to a stop inches from the lip of a bluff that sliced off into a dry gully, 40 feet straight down. Don Lavanty, peering over the edge, said, "Willy must be praying for us like crazy."

Nobody laughed. In the light of day, there was nothing funny about coming so close to killing ourselves. And as we stood there, mouths dry, heads aching, we knew there was nothing funny about breaking into that house either.

Years later, whenever we talked about THE TRIP, we glossed over that part. It was nothing to be proud of. But we learned something from the episode that helped us grow up: no matter how old you are, you are not an adult until you can behave responsibly without supervision.

We found a place where we could wash up and have breakfast. Afterward, we drove out to a nice beach, where we swam and threw a tennis ball around for a while. Then we stretched out and fell asleep, and didn't wake up until the sun had almost set. All of us were sunburned to an aching red, but John Lattanzio and Demps were in bad shape.

Big watery blisters had formed on their shoulders. I felt John's forehead, and it was really hot. Demps looked swollen all over. The words *sun poisoning* and *sunstroke* banged against my brain.

We were all scared. We found a hospital, and I pulled up to the emergency entrance. By then we practically had to carry in Demps and John.

People in white uniforms took them from us, put them in wheelchairs and whisked them away. A nurse at the desk started asking us a lot of questions. Then a doctor came out. He said our friends had been put to bed and were being treated, but they were pretty sick boys.

The doctor and the nurse then fell into a deep conversation. Someone whispered, "Let's get out of here," and we began edging toward the exit. Maybe we all heard the same inner voice at the same time, but it was Don Lavanty who spoke up: "Wait a minute. We can't just run off and leave our buddies here, sick, dying for all we know."

We slunk into the waiting room. We were nervous wrecks, agonizing over Demps and John, ready to spend the night there—until they sent us "home" with assurances that our friends were sleeping, and that there wouldn't be any more news about them until morning.

So that's how we wound up sleeping in the church basement, after all. We put in a restless night and planned to go back to the hospital the next morning. We also had to figure out whether we should call their families. Nobody wanted to be responsible for a long-distance phone call that would scare somebody's parents to death.

Don said, "Maybe we should tell them."

"Why?" asked Ronnie.

"Well, what if something—bad—happens?"

"Shut up," I said.

I could not get it out of my head that John and Demps were doing penance for all our sins of the past couple of days.

When Father Witt strode into the church basement the next morning, we flew to him. I don't think we knew until that second how hard we were hoping for him to get there, how much we counted on him. There was a babble of greetings, and then we told him the worst, that John and Demps were hospitalized with serious sunburns.

When we got to the hospital, he went to the desk, and in 15 seconds he was on his way upstairs. We didn't take our eyes off the elevator door. We knew when he came back we'd be able to tell everything just from his expression.

We got a grin. John and Demps were out of danger and would be discharged the next day. In a torrent of confession, we poured out the details of our binge—the drinking, the squandered money. We tried to edge past the episode in Dempsey's relatives' house. "We were sure they would have invited us to stay if they'd been home, Father," I said.

"It's called breaking and entering," he answered sternly. "You'll all be a long time with your next confessor, won't you?"

Suddenly he stopped in his tracks, and we milled around him, braced for the sermon. But Willy was never one to be taken for granted. "What do you want?" he asked abruptly. "A lecture you can listen to politely and promptly forget? So you can put the whole episode behind you? Well, I'm not going to accommodate you. I'd rather it worried you for a while. Maybe you can reflect on how you'd like it if a gang broke into *your* house. Do you understand me?"

We certainly did. We had let him down, and having that load of guilt was a lot worse than a bawling-out.

Willy'd had an adventure too.

Even before reaching his friend, he'd met a man named Flynn on the plane north and told him about our pilgrimage. Well, it seemed that Mr. Flynn owned a big West Coast business and lived on an estate in Hollywood. He invited Father and his altar boys to come and spend a week with him there.

Bernard F. Flynn and his wife welcomed us as if Father Witt were king, and we his princes. We had never seen a house like theirs. Our quarters were the library wing, an enormous galleried room with a wall of French windows, and a private suite at the far end for Father. The French windows opened out on a courtyard with a swimming pool.

We spent the next two days in the pool. Mrs. Flynn cooked us one fabulous meal after another and, between meals, brought us cookies and cold drinks. The Flynns shook up a lot of our preconceptions.

All we'd ever known about the rich had been filtered through the us-against-them mind-set of working-class Youngstown: hard-hearted mill owners who said no to every request of the work force; hard-hearted bankers who took pleasure in turning down loan applications. You made jokes about the rich. Rich people were from another planet.

Bernard Flynn did not fit that description. Every night he came to the library and got down on his knees with us to pray. Kind, decent and full of humility, the Flynns first led us to suspect that the images we'd been carrying around about the rich were phony caricatures. We behaved ourselves all week. No swearing. We said "Please" and "Thank you." And we made sure Stevie didn't swipe anything.

Our last four days were a sightseeing spree—Disneyland, Hollywood and a concert at the Hollywood Bowl. I can't say we all became enamored of classical music, but looking around the huge, filled amphitheater, we had to agree there must be something to it.

On Saturday, July 27, we started back east, this time taking the southern route. When we got to Las Vegas, Willy ran into George Gobel.

"Father, you know George Gobel?" Ronnie asked. "Lonesome George" Gobel, the comedian, was not only a big TV star, he also happened to be headlining the show at the Riviera.

"Now that we've chatted, I do," he replied, meaning he had walked up and introduced himself. "He's invited us to be his guests at dinner and the 8 p.m. show."

We could only gape with amazement at how he kept topping himself. Scrubbed and dressed in our road-worn best, we were fed a steak dinner and even introduced to the audience. "We have eight altar boys from Youngstown, Ohio, and their priest with us tonight," George Gobel announced, and we stood up to a big round of applause. "So we had to rewrite the whole show," he added.

Everyone laughed, Willy barely. By now he had seen some of the showgirls, each one more gorgeous than the other. I noticed Father checking us nervously from time to time.

We boys had two adjoining rooms at the motel, and Father was down the hall. As soon as we said our prayers, and he bade us good night, all eight of us began itemizing reasons why it was ridiculous to be going to sleep when all Las Vegas was out there, when all those girls who'd smiled so prettily at us . . .

We waited a few minutes to make sure Father was tucked in, then gently turned the doorknob and pushed. The door, which opened to the outside, went about six inches and ran smack into the Cadillac. "Who the hell did that?" someone asked, already knowing the answer. A rush for the other room, but then came the sad dawning that the venture was doomed. Sure enough, the other door opened only as far as the first.

And so it all came clear: Willy, who knew more about what was in our heads than we ever gave him credit for, had quietly shut us in and gone off to a sound sleep.

It was our last attempt to kick over the traces. We rolled on, to Flagstaff, Arizona, where we blew a tire, and all rushed out to make sure nothing serious had happened to our Caddy. By this time we knew she was not only our transportation but our refuge. The powerful purr of that engine was reassurance we'd get home. We drove on to Gallup, New Mexico, and stayed on an Indian Reservation near there; then north into Colorado and east to Kansas.

A kind of calm had settled on us. We didn't smoke as much anymore. I suppose part of it was plain fatigue from five weeks on the road. But mostly it was the dawning realization that THE TRIP was a watershed in our lives. Nothing was as it had been before; none of the things we'd taken for granted were firmly in place anymore. If Youngstown wasn't the whole world—and now we knew that it was not—then whatever aspirations we had were not limited by the kind of future Youngstown had to offer. We did not have to follow in our fathers' footsteps.

Our moral horizons has opened outward too. The Bible and the Ten Commandments remained the foundation of our faith, but in those weeks on the road, Father had helped us see that faith didn't mean much if it was compartmentalized in our lives. "You'd be better off believing that God doesn't exist at all than believing he only turns up for special occasions, like Mass or funerals," he told us. Religious faith was an everyday matter.

You couldn't shrug him off, because he made you think. Faith took courage, he said, because you had to be brave to believe in something you couldn't see or touch or put in the bank. But this mystery's very intangibility filled it with excitement and challenge.

And reward. Did we think it was the tooth fairy that had called Father to Northern California, leaving us to fail our first test of self-reliance but learn the larger truth about growing up? Didn't we recognize the hand of the Almighty?

A warm sense of belonging took hold of us. Everybody wants to *belong*, and it felt good to be committed to our faith and to one another. We knew by then that even though life might scatter us to the far corners of the earth, this experience that we shared would hold us together always.

Somewhere along the way we also came to understand that the ability to throw or hit or kick a ball was not the ultimate measure of a man. One night in St. Louis I heard Ronnie and John asking Willy questions about college. Could they get in? How much was tuition?

We crossed Illinois and Indiana and were back in Ohio. The steel mills glowed in the sky up ahead. We were home.

People made a big fuss over us. The *Vindicator* had a story about the trip, and we were all interviewed on WFMJ-TV. Florence Miller threw a fancy lawn party for us.

Three months before, we would have gorged ourselves on Mrs. Miller's food and stood around making crude remarks about her guests. But that was in another lifetime. Now we were polite, reasonably friendly—and we made our parents very proud.

Then the summer was over, and we were back in the real world. For some of us it was our senior year; we were supposed to start looking for jobs. But the real world was not the one we had left a lifetime ago. Nothing was the same, not school, not the neighborhood and especially not ourselves. To have a new car was still appealing, but was it worth committing yourself to a future with a dead end? We were fresh from seeing another world, other possibilities.

It wasn't a matter of getting to be as wealthy as the Flynns or Mrs. Miller, but what was wrong with aiming higher than the steel mills? Or trying to reach the level of decency and kindness shown to us by those people who, only a little while before, we would have written off as rich folks who cared only for their own?

We spent a lot of time talking to Willy. George said he wanted to study music, but there were already plenty of unemployed musicians.

"Do what you love, George," Father told him. "You'll make a living." And George enrolled as a music major at Youngstown University.

John and Ron signed up, and then I did too. Instead of a new car, I bought a $50 wreck of a Plymouth. When I couldn't afford to pay the insurance premium, it sat in the driveway, and I hitchhiked to school. "Never mind," said Father. "You've got a future."

Don Lavanty was granted a scholarship by the University of Dayton. Jim Dempsey started at Youngstown University a couple of years later. We were breaking the mold—just as our fathers and grandfathers had done when they came to America.

All except Stevie. He graduated from East High in 1960. But whatever it was that had hold of him held him in a vise. One day he heard me moaning about paying $20 for a college textbook. The next day he brought one to me.

"Stevie, where did you get this book?" I asked him.

"What's the difference? You said you needed it. I got it for you."

"There's a big difference. Stevie, things that don't belong to you are not yours for the taking."

"Dammit, are you ever gonna quit leaning on me?" he said. He walked off, and I had to resort to a feat of reverse shoplifting to get the book back into the store.

Stevie is not present at our 35th reunion, which is hard to believe, because he was so much a part of us. In a sense, THE TRIP was Stevie's last chance, and he let it get away. For a long time I wondered if we had failed him—were we too hard on him, or too easy? But Father Witt said Stevie listened to voices that no one else heard, and that none of us— or anyone in his life—ever did reach him.

Over the years, he started drinking heavily. He fought it off, then lost out. On a spring day in 1981, at age 38, he was found in his apartment, dead of a heart attack.

The slides keep flicking by, the last tangible evidence of our great adventure. George's diary disappeared, and so did John's letters to his long-ago girlfriend. As for all the pictures I took with my Kodak Hawkeye, hardly any of them turned out. "Did you ever wonder about that?" Stevie asked me years afterward.

I shrugged. "I just thought it was me."

"It was me," he said, laughing. "Every time you rapped me on the head I opened the back of your camera and exposed the film."

Our August 1992 reunion is not complete until 10 p.m., when the doorbell rings. Father Witt comes bustling in, full of apologies he doesn't need to make because we all know he has been off somewhere doing God's work. At age 70 he is in his 34th year of broadcasting a regular radio program and keeps his door wide open to any who need his counsel, support, sympathy or maybe $10 until payday.

Few of us have a dearer friend. When Don Lavanty was struggling to pay his tuition at George Washington University Law School, Father got him a scholarship and a job on the Capitol police force. When George Bonamase lost his eldest son in an accident ten years ago, Father was there for him until he could cope. He has touched every one of us.

We all still live in Youngstown, or within a few hundred miles. But of course it's not the same city. The steel mills have long since shut down, and a lot of the guys we grew up with are scattered. Some did time in jail. We will always wonder what we would be doing now if THE TRIP hadn't elevated our aspirations.

Not one of us has lost his faith. Nor have we forgotten what Father Witt told us about paying back the gifts that made THE TRIP possible.

When Father Witt became pastor of a nearby parish that was in desperate need of a new church, we were there with our hearts and our checkbooks. We became surrogate godfathers to one another's kids—what do you need? a job? a loan? a place to live?—and the circle fanned out to include our kids' friends, and their friends, until a kind of Father Witt alumni association that sometimes seems to encompass the whole world knows where to turn in a pinch.

Don Lavanty is now a lawyer. George Bonamase is a school band director. Jim Barone, a painting contractor, has gone back to college and has almost completed his degree. Jim Dempsey is still something of a loner; he is a constant reader, an eternal student, a happy man.

Ron Guerrieri owns an advertising agency. John Lattanzio started as a shoe clerk, discovered a flair for selling, and 15 years later became the company president, responsible for 700 stores.

I divide my time between Europe, where I am managing director of a manufacturing company, and the home office in Youngstown, where I am a group vice president. Sometimes on my way to work, I drive through the old neighborhood, past the red-brick church where it all began. And every day I'm in Youngstown, I spend a minute looking out my office window over bare remnants of the steel mills, and on up to the old neighborhood, reminding myself, Bob Calcagni, where I am and where I came from.

We watch the final slides go by, brushing tears of laughter and deeper emotion from our eyes. And long after the lights go on we are still journeying westward. We can never forget our pilgrimage, our voyage of discovery, the time we found our true selves.

SOME THINGS YOU JUST KNOW

BY

W. W. MEADE

When my son was small, he liked to sit on my lap and watch television. Sometimes he'd point out what was in the real world—auto accidents, fires, Joe Montana, astronauts—and what was not. Big Bird, for instance, belonged to the world of make-believe, as did Kermit the Frog and the Grinch. But so did dinosaurs.

Luke had trouble understanding dinosaurs. My explanation that they once were real but existed no more perplexed and annoyed him. If they weren't around now, then they never had been, and that was that.

One day Mawmaw, his great-grandmother, sent him a drawing of a cat she had done. Enclosed was a note that suggested he color it. She often sent him small projects, and he dearly loved getting letters from her. He finished his project and then climbed into my chair to show it to me. It was red and blue and green.

"I've never seen such a colorful cat," I said.

"'Course not, Dad," he said. "It's mine an' Mawmaw's," as though that somehow explained things. He nestled against me, and I clicked on the TV to a retrospective of the life of John Kennedy.

As a picture of young JFK at the tiller of a small sailboat appeared, Luke asked, "Who is that man?"

"It's John Kennedy. He was the President of the United States."

"Where is he now?"

"He's dead."

"He's not dead. He's running the boat." The image changed, and we saw JFK giving his inaugural address. "See, there he is some more."

"Well, that was a long time ago. He's dead now, Luke."

My son looked into my face to see if I was teasing. "Is he all dead?"

"Yes."

"His feet dead?"

"Yes."

"His head dead?"

"Yes."

This last question was followed by a long, thoughtful pause. Then he said, "Well, he certainly speaks very well."

Although I tried not too, I laughed, because he had been so earnest in examining the problem.

After the JFK incident, Luke seemed haunted by the problem of death and dying. Thereafter, almost every walk in the woods became a search for a dead field mouse or raccoon or bird. He would squat down over the find and make up stories about what the animal had been doing when it died. Sometimes we held small funerals.

I was concerned, of course. The idea of death was a big thing for a three-year-old to get a handle on.

One day in the woods we found a few tawny tufts of rabbit fur. Luke touched them with a sassafras twig. "This was Peter Rabbit," he said finally. "He was going home to his dinner. A fox ate him up. He is in a fox now."

"But Peter Rabbit is in the world of make-believe," I said. "This was a real rabbit."

"I know that," he said. "I was just *seeing*."

I think he meant he was making up a story that would somehow let things turn out better.

Most people, I explained, thought only your body died—that another part, called a spirit, survived. We didn't know that for sure, I said. But if you believed something deep inside, even though you couldn't prove it, that was called faith.

This produced amazement and an inquiry that lasted almost a week. On one of our walks I showed him a butterfly cocoon that had once housed a pupa. I told him that a caterpillar had spun a cocoon and eventually had become a butterfly. He accepted that easily because he had seen it on a nature show.

Then he said, "But you can still see the real butterfly. He goes places. You can touch him. If you're dead, people can only see you on TV."

"That's true," I said. "But you can still see them in your head—in your imagination."

He thought long and hard about that one. Finally he asked me how that could be. I told him to close his eyes and imagine someone who was not with us. His best friend, Charlie, for instance.

"Can you imagine him?" I asked.

He squealed with delight. "No. But I can hear him!"

"Well, it's like that. People who aren't with you right at the moment sort of hang around with you for as long as you remember them."

"But I can play with Charlie. I couldn't go play with the bunny. Because he's dead."

"Yes. That's right."

For another few days Luke's preoccupation with dead things continued. But then his attention switched to his upcoming birthday party, and he did not speak of his deep concern again.

About a year and a half later Mawmaw died. It is our Southern family's custom to lay our kin out at home, so my father's mother had a wake. When Luke insisted he be allowed to go, my wife and I thought this to be a good idea.

Mawmaw's house was overflowing with guests and food and talk. She had lived a long rich life, so there was none of the wretched grief that comes with early or unexpected deaths. People remembered her joy in life, her amazing personal strength, her humor and kindness.

We did not ask Luke if he wanted to go into the room where she lay. We let him do as he pleased—talking to people, eating, getting praised and playing with cousins. Then, at almost the last possible moment, he asked to see Mawmaw.

I took his hand and led him to stand beside his great-grandmother's bier. He was too small to see anything but flowers, so I picked him up. He took a long look and then said, "Okay, Dad."

I put him down, and we walked out of the room and down the hallway toward the kitchen. Before we got there, he pulled me into a small room where my grandmother used to press flowers or do needlework. Looking solemnly at me, he whispered, "Dad, that's not Mawmaw."

"What do you mean?"

"It isn't," he said. "She's not in there."

"Then where is she?" I asked.

"Talking somewhere."

"Why do you think that?"

"I don't think it. I know it."

"How do you know?"

"I just know. That's it. I just know." There was a long pause as we looked at each other, face to face. Finally he said, "Is that faith?"

"Yes, Luke. That's faith."

"Well, then that's what I got," he said.

I looked at him with awe and joy. I knew he had just found one of the most powerful resources of the heart—a guide other than his mother or me. He had found a way of understanding that would be with him for the rest of his life, even in the valley of the shadow of death.

The animated voices of family and friends drifted toward us from the kitchen, where a lavish buffet was arranged on Mawmaw's long oak table. They were sharing stories of the extraordinary woman we all loved so dearly. I looked at Luke smiling up at me, and then we walked down the hall, hand in hand, to get some fried chicken. And to tell a story or two.

Nothing in this world is so marvelous as

the transformation that a soul undergoes

when the light of faith descends upon

the light of reason.

W. BERNARD ULLATHORNE

"DON'T LET MY BABY DIE"

BY

SAMUEL A. SCHREINER, JR.

*S*ean Kroll, 2½, edged quietly into the bathroom where his mother was busy drying her hair. Pointing toward the kitchen, he mumbled, "Jennifer . . . in the water." *She has probably squirted water on the floor from the drinking-water dispenser again,* thought Tammy Kroll, annoyed by the possibility of another mopping up.

Hurrying into the kitchen, she noticed the back door was open. One-year-old Jennifer was nowhere in sight. *What's going on?* she wondered. Sean had never unlocked a door before.

Panic began to grip her as she ran out onto the deck leading to an above-ground pool. No Jennifer—anywhere. *My God! The pool,* Tammy thought. The water was only four feet deep, but it was dirty from the long winter and she could see nothing below the murky surface. Without thinking, Tammy plunged into the ice-cold water. To her horror, a tiny body in a red dress floated up. It was Jennifer.

Tammy grabbed the lifeless form and clambered out of the pool. She felt for Jennifer's pulse. None. She checked for breathing. None.

Jennifer's fingers and lips were blue; her arms slopped like a rag doll's. "Jennifer, baby!"

With the limp child in her arms, Tammy ran to the kitchen, picked up the wall phone just inside the door and punched "O" for operator. The phone rang and rang. *C'mon, c'mon!* she pleaded. More ringing. Finally, a crisp recorded voice came on the line: "Due to a work stoppage, we are unable to handle your call immediately . . ." Tammy slammed down the receiver.

CPR, she thought, laying Jennifer out on the kitchen deck. Cardiopulmonary resuscitation. *Gotta get oxygen into Jennifer!* From her high-school CPR instructor, Tammy knew every second counted. She clamped her mouth over her daughter's tiny nose and mouth. *Blow. Pause. Blow. Pause.* Then, lifting her head, Tammy screamed for help.

On the street behind the Krolls' suburban Chicago house, James Patridge, a blond, bearded 38-year-old, drew a deep breath in the brisk morning air. It was good to be alive—he was always thankful for that. Twenty years before, in Vietnam, both of his legs had been blown off just above the knee. He was also left blind in one eye, and nearly blind in the other.

Reaching for a garbage bag to haul out to the street on the footrest of his wheelchair, James heard a faint scream. He squinted toward the distant sound, then dropped the bag and raced his wheelchair down the driveway. He wheeled across the road and onto the bumpy surface of an open lot. There he paused and listened. This time the woman's cry, almost a death wail, seemed closer. It went through him like a current.

Just like the screams on that day in Vietnam: March 31, 1966, somewhere near Da Nang. James was point man as his Marine platoon headed across a grassy field. Suddenly, a booby trap exploded, mortally wounding the men just behind him. The force sent him flying into the air. Somewhere close by, a buddy was screaming, "Don't let me die."

157

Legless and legally blind, James Patridge now lived on his full-disability support from the Veterans Administration. Two sons from his first marriage resided nearby with their mother. In 1981 he had married Sue Fowler and adopted her young son. James spent most of his time working at occasional odd jobs and playing with his boys.

"James . . . James!" It was Sue, calling from behind. Her voice was getting closer. He didn't pause to look back. James pushed harder at the wheels. Small rocks and sticks slowed him down. Despite the morning chill, sweat streamed down his forehead and chest.

"Where are you?" he yelled to the woman's voice ahead. "Tell me where you are!"

The screaming stopped. "Over here! This way!"

Now Sue was beside him.

"Can you see anything?" James asked her.

"No, there's a hedge up ahead—small trees so close you can't see through them." Sue was terrified. The screams were garbled, and she thought she heard "Don't rape me!" That could mean a gun or a knife.

But Sue knew nothing would stop James. There was little he couldn't or wouldn't do, when he put his mind to it. Fix the car. Mow the lawn. Wrestle his sons to the floor. He had covered the 80 yards across the lot in only minutes.

James had learned determination early. Growing up on a farm near Clay City in southern Illinois, he was the youngest of six children who worked hard for everything they got. In high school, James decided to be a Marine—and that was it. He graduated on a Friday in May 1965 and was in boot camp in San Diego the following Monday.

As another scream tore the air, James rolled out of his wheelchair onto the ground, squirmed through four to five feet of tangled brush and hoisted himself onto his hands. Then, swinging his body through his arms, he raced forward on his hands toward the house. *Gotta get there quick!* he thought, taking longer, faster strides with each arm.

It was 75 feet from the brush to the Krolls' house. Sue bounded up the eight wooden steps from the lawn to the kitchen deck.

Pushing with his stumps and heaving with his hands, James scrambled up the steps.

"Don't let my baby die," Tammy screamed.

Die of what? James wondered. *What's going on?*

Looking up, Tammy saw a woman running toward her across the deck. "Call an ambulance!" she pleaded. To Sue the child looked dead. She was blue all over. Her eyes were rolled back. Sue felt sick.

"James, should I dial O or 911?"

"Better try 911," James said. His voice was calm as he came sliding across the deck. He moved to Tammy's side so quickly that she didn't notice he had no legs.

James felt for a pulse in the baby's neck. There was none. He touched her skin. It held an icy chill that he had learned to recognize on the battlefield—the cold touch of death. *How long has she been dead?* he thought. He realized that even if she were revived, every second without oxygen increased the chances of brain damage.

With God all things are possible.

MATTHEW 19

As he squinted close-up, James could now see that Tammy was doing the CPR wrong. Ten years before, he had taken a CPR course. It was only a way of passing time. After all, how often would a legless man have to save someone's life? James remembered the first rule of resuscitation: open the airways. James took the child from Tammy and, tilting her head back, checked for breathing. Finding none, he attempted unsuccessfully to breathe air into her. To clear the blocked air passages, he gently pressed her stomach. Water spouted from the baby's mouth and nose. He placed the child on her back and began the rhythmic breathe-press technique of CPR.

Between breaths, James talked softly to Jennifer, urging the child back to life. Then, far off, he heard sirens, but only because he had been listening for them and had inwardly been praying for them. Now he knew help was coming. At last. *Breathe, push-count . . . breathe, push-count . . .*

As the sirens grew louder, James suddenly felt a slight quiver, a gasp for air. "She's trying to breathe," he told Tammy. "I've got a heartbeat!" The beats, however, were irregular and faint. So James continued the CPR, ignoring everything but the wispy flutter of life in his hands. Then suddenly he was aware of people rushing up and kneeling beside him and the baby.

The first to arrive were Captain William Enders and firefighter Peter Daly, emergency medical technicians with the Winfield Fire Protection District. They suctioned the baby's air passages and held a mask attached to an oxygen bottle over her tiny face. Jennifer *was* breathing!

Shortly, paramedics Michael Turner and Kelly Kindelin of the Leonard Ambulance Service came running onto the deck. They checked the baby's pulse. It was only 50 beats a minute, compared with an infant's normal rate of 100. When Turner tried to insert an intravenous tube, Jennifer cried out.

James felt the tension break. "She's okay; she's going to make it," Sue said to him quietly.

After the ambulance left, James slowly slide himself over to the steps and eased down them one at a time. Then, hoisting himself once more onto his hands, he swung his tired body into his wheelchair. Minutes later, he was back in his garage, loading garbage bags. It promised to be a good day.

At the Central Du Page Hospital, Jennifer made a rapid recovery. The cold pool water had protected her from brain damage. James Patridge's CPR had done the rest.

After Tammy Kroll and her husband, Michael, told the story of how their neighbor had saved Jennifer's life, newspapers and television stations all over the country turned James Patridge into a national hero. Phone calls poured into his home from well-wishers. Many were from fellow Vietnam veterans who took understandable pride in what he had done. One call came from organizers of a Vietnam veterans march scheduled for Flag Day celebrations. They wanted James to serve as an honorary marshal of the parade and to lead the march through the streets of Chicago.

A private man, James tended to shun organizations. But he agreed to join the march because, he said, he still believed in the cause for which he lost his legs and most of his sight in Vietnam. But he turned down many other honors, gifts and requests for appearances; he wanted to get back to the quiet life he had enjoyed before.

Two days after Jennifer's near-drowning, a grateful Michael and Tammy Kroll stopped by James Patridge's house. The couple were bringing Jennifer home. Gently Michael placed Jennifer in James's arms. He cradled her close, talking softly to her.

Something happened that morning of the rescue that James Patridge had trouble explaining. "Let me put it this way," he said. "When a human being dies—and Jennifer *was* dead—a mortal man like myself can do nothing." Even though he did not consider himself a religious man, James felt he was an instrument for a greater presence. All the Krolls knew was that they had lost their infant daughter that morning—and James Patridge was there to bring her back to life. For them, that is explanation enough.

Faith is knowing there is an ocean because you have seen a brook.

WILLIAM ARTHUR WARD

UNFORGETTABLE JANE EDNA HILL

BY

REVEREND EDWARD VICTOR HILL

On the day before we were to wed, Jane Edna Coruthers took my hand and rushed me into the backyard of her parents' home in Prairie View, Texas. All summer long Texas farmers had vainly prayed for rain. The sunbaked earth was dry and cracked. Crops were scorched. Lawns were dead brown.

"Come on, Edward," she said, looking over her shoulder with a smile. "See how the pampas is going to bloom for us!"

Since childhood, Jane had dreamed of an outdoor wedding in a field of flowers. She had planted a large clump of pampas grass in her parents' yard, confident that one day she would say her vows beneath its regal, white plumes. Now our marriage ceremony was just a day away, but Jane's eyes sparkled with hope as she stood before the dry, withered stems.

"Any moment," she said, taking a tightly rolled pod in her hand, "they're going to open!"

Doctor John Milton Coruthers, Jane's father, walked up behind us. A distinguished professor of agriculture at Prairie View College, he could tell you scientifically why that sun-parched clump of pampas would not bloom for Jane's wedding. But he simply smiled—he was too wise to question his daughter's faith.

At about noon the next day, August 29, 1955, lightning suddenly flashed and thunder pealed in the distance. I stood shock-silent, staring at the sky as black clouds boiled up and tiny drops of rain stirred the dust at our feet. Jane laughed and lifted up her hands in praise. "We plant the seed," she whispered, "but God makes it grow."

I don't know when Jane first read that ancient Biblical promise, but it shaped her life. She believed, with all her heart, that she and God together could do almost anything.

Three hours later, the summer storm stopped. As Jane and I pledged our sacred vows, the majestic pampas flowers waved above us in the breeze.

In the years that followed, while I pastored first in Houston and then at the Mount Zion Missionary Baptist Church of Los Angeles, Jane always tended her gardens. No backyard plot was too rocky or dry for her to plant, weed and prune.

And no human heart was too hard, no body too worn for her to cultivate. With an invitation to lunch or a gesture to sit beside her in the pastor's pew, with a late-night phone call or a word of encouragement, Jane—we all called her "Baby"—planted seeds of love in all of us.

One cold fall evening soon after our marriage, I returned to our little home and opened the door to a blaze of burning candles. Baby hugged me and announced, "We've been married six months, and I thought we'd eat by candlelight."

I discovered candles burning in the kitchen and bedroom. When I tried to flick on the bathroom lights, I understood the reason for our romantic meal. I found Jane in the kitchen, and she began to cry.

"They turned off our electricity," she said, reaching out to hug me, knowing how terrible I would feel. In college Jane had been courted by heirs of the rich and famous, but she had chosen me, a poor Baptist preacher. Now I couldn't even pay the light bill.

"You work so hard," she said, holding me tight. "With or without money, I love you and I respect your calling. Wherever we are together, we are rich."

Jane's candlelight dinner was just another way of tending her garden. Since she worked as a nurse, church-choir member, Sunday-school teacher, volunteer counselor and community leader, it wasn't just family that she nurtured.

Mark Chiles was 15 years old when he met "Aunt Jane," his new Sunday-school teacher. Because he stuttered, some parishioners assumed he was retarded. He sat in the back row, hoping no one would notice him.

But Jane noticed. She listened intently to him and discovered that he was quite bright. She invited him to sit with her in church, a place of honor in our congregation. She helped him with his speech therapy, and when he was selected for the Job Corps, she slipped him a little money to get him through the long, hot summer in South Dakota.

In December 1989, as one of our young-adult ministers, the boy who once hid in the last pew of the Mount Zion Church preached from its pulpit. "I looked out at the congregation," Mark told me, "and I could almost hear Auntie Jane whisper, 'You can do it, Mark. You can do it.'"

Joe Jackson was another young life that Jane tended. "God has a dream for your life, boy," she told the 13-year-old, getting down on her knees and grasping Joe's thin shoulders. "And I am going to see that God's dream for you comes true."

Jane's love took root in him and grew. In an area where drugs and gangs abounded, Joe never became involved. Today he is a policeman and a member of our church.

Baby's toughness saved a lot of people from grief—including me. When members of a militant group called to threaten my life for my outspoken stand against them, Jane got the call. Though most of her ancestors were African slaves, Baby was part American Indian. She told the surprised militants what might happen to them if they "got this tough Indian lady on the warpath."

When one late-night caller said I didn't have long to live, Jane was concerned a bomb might have been planted in my car. Rather than disturb me, she simply got up early to test the car herself. "Don't worry," she said when I found her in the garage. "There was no bomb."

In 1986, every Thursday morning at 6:30, Jane and our son, Edward II, joined other volunteers serving breakfast to hundreds of transients and neighbors at the soup kitchen we founded, The Lord's Kitchen. We always asked the hungry patrons their names and tried to greet each one courteously. But one huge middle-aged woman on her first visit refused to cooperate.

"I'm Pippi Longstocking," she snapped. Her voice echoed about the room, and no one dared challenge her. Her face was dirty and scarred, her clothes were torn, and she swaggered like a drunk.

"I'm Snow White," she answered the second day. On Wednesday she was "Ronald Reagan," and on Thursday, Jane's day on duty, she growled, "I'm Jesus Christ. Don't mess with me!"

The woman was used to getting her own way. She just hadn't reckoned on Baby. "Listen, sweetheart," my wife replied firmly, "your name isn't Jesus Christ. I happen to know that man personally, and he doesn't look anything like you."

The room grew silent. Even the cooks and dishwashers stopped to see what would happen as the bag lady just stared at Jane with angry, flashing eyes. Suddenly, the woman balled her callused hands into fists.

"You are a good person," Jane said quietly. "These people may think you're mean or dangerous, but I know you're not."

My son got ready to dive under the table and pull his mother after him. Nobody in The Lord's Kitchen could believe that the pastor's wife would confront this she-mountain.

"You're angry," Jane continued evenly. "Life has been unfair to you. But you're not the only person suffering in this place. So why don't you wipe that frown off your face, use this towel to wash yourself in the bathroom, and come back here and sit beside me. I'll pour us an extra cup of coffee and we'll talk."

Suddenly that tough-looking woman began to cry.

"My name is Elizabeth," she whispered, collapsing like a frightened child into my wife's arms.

"And my name is Jane," Baby answered, holding her new friend for a moment while everybody—cooks, dishwashers and patrons alike—applauded and wiped away their tears.

Elizabeth regularly spent Thursday mornings with Jane at The Lord's Kitchen. Jane never told me what they talked about, but the scowl on Elizabeth's face gave way to a smile.

While I was busy helping organize the civil-rights movement, Baby avoided the spotlight to care for her ever-growing family. She sent cards to encourage friends and strangers. She telephoned to pass on words of comfort to those reeling from the horrors of brutality. She prayed without ceasing for everyone on her list. She never made the headlines, but none of the "important folks" I've known, the famous, the leaders, could outshine my own dear Jane Edna Hill.

Faith is to believe what you do not yet see; the reward for this faith is to see what you believe.

SAINT AUGUSTINE

168

Then, in 1985, Baby developed a nasty cough. Microscopic cancers were growing in her lungs. The family prayed, cried and watched helplessly as our beloved wife and mother became weaker each day.

From the intensive chemotherapy treatment Baby suffered a severe and constant pain in her left shoulder. Yet she continued to work for "Baby's bad boys," as she called the young men she had taken under her wing.

On October 28, 1987, her courageous battle ended, and Jane Edna Coruthers Hill went home to be with the Lord. On the day we buried her, 3000 mourners came to the church, black and white together.

I sat on the platform looking down at that great congregation who had come to say good-bye to Baby. "Don't cry for me, Edward," Jane had told me just before she died. "Look how many seeds we've planted together and how many flowers are already in bloom."

In that huge crowd were hundreds of people whose lives had been touched by her simple faithfulness. And scattered among them I could see dozens of "Baby's bad boys." Once they had faced addiction, prison terms and violent death. Now they stood there with tears streaming down their faces, reaching out to touch the casket of the woman who had helped them live. Twelve of them insisted on carrying Baby's casket through the grieving throng.

On a cold, drizzling morning after Baby passed away, I was hurrying to my car and noticed a young woman and her baby bundled in rags. They were trying to sleep on the pavement.

As I stood blinking back the rain, trying to focus on that dirty pile of rags, I felt Jane standing with me. "Look, Edward," she would have said, rushing to the mother and child.

Jane would know what I was thinking. How hard we had tried and how often we had failed to make a dent in the desperate needs of our neighborhood alone. But kneeling beside that cold and hungry little family, Jane would have insisted that we try again.

"We just plant the seed. . . ." Her voice echoed in my heart.

I could see Jane picking up the baby and leading the homeless, teenage mother to refuge. There would be no discussion. The girl and her child were in need. There was nothing more to say.

As I helped the young mother and her baby into my car, I suddenly knew there was something more God and Jane would have me do. The congregation had raised money to replace our cramped church with a new, larger building. Instead, we would have to provide a home for women and infants who need food and temporary shelter.

When I told the people of Mount Zion the story of that young woman and her child and proposed the shelter, the congregation lifted their hands in praise to God. The vote was unanimous.

Called The Jane Edna Hill Home for Women and Infants, it will be a garden to tend fragile roots so young flowers can blossom into life.

"Thank you, heavenly Father," I hear Jane say. "We planted the seeds, but You have made them grow."

If you have faith as a grain of mustard
seed, you will say to this mountain, "Move
hence to yonder place" and it will move;
and nothing will be impossible to you.

MATTHEW 17

BECAUSE OF ADAM

BY

HENRI J. M. NOUWEN

Recently I moved from Harvard to a place near Toronto called
Daybreak—that is, from an institution for the best and the brightest to
a community where mentally handicapped people and their assistants
try to live together in the spirit of the Beatitudes. In my house, ten of
us form a family. Gradually I am forgetting who is handicapped and
who is not. We are simply John, Bill, Trevor, Raymond, Rose, Steve, Jane,
Naomi, Henri . . . and Adam. I want to tell you Adam's story.

Adam is the weakest person of our family. He is a 25-year-old man
who cannot speak, dress himself, walk or eat without help. His back is
curved, and his arm and leg movements are spastic. He suffers from
severe epilepsy, and even with heavy medication he has few days without grand-mal seizures.

It takes me about an hour and a half to wake Adam, give him his
medication, undress him, carry him into his bath, wash him, shave him,
clean his teeth, dress him, walk him to the kitchen, give him breakfast,
put him in his wheelchair and bring him to the place where he spends
most of the day doing therapeutic exercises. When a seizure occurs, this

sequence of activities takes more time, and often Adam has to return to sleep to regain his energy.

I tell you all of this not to give you a nursing report but to share with you something quite intimate. After a month of working with Adam something started to happen to me that never had happened before. This severely handicapped young man, whom outsiders sometimes describe with very hurtful words, started to become my dearest companion. As my fears of entering Adam's unfamiliar world gradually decreased, I began to feel a profound tenderness and affection toward him. My other tasks seemed boring and superficial compared with the hours I spent with Adam. Out of his broken body and broken mind he offered me a greater gift than I would ever be able to offer him.

As I carried him into his bath and made waves to let the water run fast around him and told him all sorts of stories, I knew that two friends were communicating far beyond the realm of thought. Before this, I had come to believe that what makes us human is our mind. But Adam keeps showing me that what makes us human is our heart, the center of our being, where God has hidden trust, hope and love. Deep speaks to deep, spirit speaks to spirit, heart speaks to heart. If Adam wants anything of me, it is that I simply be with him.

Whoever sees in Adam merely a burden to society misses the sacred mystery that Adam is fully capable of receiving and giving love. He is fully human, not half human, not nearly human, but fully, completely human because he is all heart. And it is our heart that is made in the image of God. The longer I stay with Adam, the more clearly I see him as a gentle teacher, teaching me what no book or professor ever could.

Most of my life I have tried to show the world that I could do it on my own. I earned degrees and awards and made my career as a theology professor. Yes, I fought my way up to a little success, a little power. But as I sit beside the slow and heavy-breathing Adam, I start seeing how

that journey was marked by rivalry and competition, and spotted with moments of suspicion, jealousy, resentment and revenge. The great paradox is that in his complete emptiness of all human pride, Adam is giving me a whole new understanding of God's love.

Once, when Adam's parents came for a visit, I asked, "Tell me, during all the years you had Adam in your home, what did he give you?" His father smiled and said without hesitation, "He brought us peace."

I know he is right. After months of being with Adam, I am discovering in myself an inner quiet that I did not know before. Adam is one of the most broken persons among us, but without any doubt our strongest bond. Because of Adam there is always someone home; because of Adam there is a quiet rhythm in the house; because of Adam there are moments of silence; because of Adam there are always words of affection and tenderness; because of Adam there is patience and endurance; because of Adam there are smiles and tears visible to all; because of Adam there is always time and space for forgiveness and healing. Yes, because of Adam there is peace among us.

Like me, you search for peace in your heart, your family and your world. But looking around us, we see kidnappings, torture, murder, calamity. As we grow older, and the peace we wait for still has not come, something in us is in danger of growing cold, despairing. And still, peace is what our hearts desire most.

Let me tell you about Adam's peace, a peace that the world cannot give. Adam can do nothing. He is completely dependent on others. Every evening when I help Adam with his supper and put him to bed, I realize that the best thing I can do for Adam is to be with him. That is my great joy: paying total attention to his breathing, his eating, his careful steps; looking at how he tries to lift a spoon to his mouth, or offers his left arm a little to make it easier to take off his shirt; always wondering about pains he cannot express but that still ask for relief.

The peace that flows from Adam is not the result of political analysis, round-table debates or well-thought-out strategies. All these activities of the mind have their role to play. But Adam's peace is rooted in the heart, and in utter weakness. Why there? Because precisely where we are weakest, where we cannot rely on our own self-sufficiency, *there* the peace that is not of this world is hidden. With this peace in our hearts, we will be able to hear with new ears the words "Blessed are the peacemakers, for they shall be called the children of God." This fills me with happiness for all the Adams of this world.

I have told you about Adam's peace to offer you a quiet guide with a gentle heart who gives you a little light to walk with through this dark world. Adam does not solve anything. Even with all the support he receives, he cannot change his own utter helplessness. It is unlikely Adam will get much better. He is extremely vulnerable. An infection, a fall or any one of many other incidents may take him suddenly away from us. When he dies, nobody will be able to boast about anything. Still, what a light he brings!

My part in Adam's life is small. Some cook for him, others do his laundry, some give him messages, others play him music, take him for rides. But the peaceful community that Adam has called forth is not there just for Adam, but for all who belong to Adam's race. It is a community that proclaims that God has chosen to descend among us in complete weakness and vulnerability. This is how he reveals his glory.

Thus, as you can see, Adam is teaching me something about the peace that is not of this world. It is a peace rooted in simply being

175

present for each other, a peace that speaks of God's love—the love that bonds us, holds us in a fellowship of the weak.

Adam has never said a word to me. He never will. But every night when I put him to bed, I say to him, "Thank you." As I cover him with blankets and turn out the lights, I pray with Adam. He is always very quiet, as if he knows that my praying voice sounds a little different from my speaking voice. It is then, as he looks up to me from his pillow, that I whisper in his ear, "May all the angels protect you."

The only faith that wears well and holds its color in all weather is that which is woven of conviction.

JAMES RUSSELL LOWELL

ME AND THE PREACHER MAN

BY
MICKEY BLOCK,
WITH WILLIAM KIMBALL

My last mission started little differently from the rest—the same routine, the same tension. It was July 1969, soon after the beginning of my second tour of duty in Vietnam. The only ones left of the original group of "Mekong Headhunters" attached to Navy SEAL Team One were a guy I'll call Buddy Mercer and myself.

Some of the new men in our unit fit in; some didn't. One particularly annoying individual we sarcastically called the Preacher Man. He bunked underneath me and strummed incessantly on his guitar, singing preachy songs and saying how much God loved us. Buddy and I would tell him to knock it off. He, in turn, referred to me as Pervert Number One and Buddy as Pervert Number Two.

We were on a night ambush, and our PBR, or patrol boat (river), was beached along the bank of a muddy brown tributary in the Mekong Delta. It had been raining, and broken veils of mist floated above the water. Overhead, clouds interrupted the moon's glow.

Unknown to us, another PBR mistakenly drifted into our ambush area. The crew was inexperienced and trigger-happy. They detected the rough outline of our boat with their night-vision scope and thought we were the enemy.

All of a sudden their guns crisscrossed our boat with thousands of armor-piercing bullets. "Get us out of here!" I yelled, thinking we were being attacked by Vietcong. A violent blast flung me backward. It felt as if someone was whipping me with a hot wire cable. I pulled myself up, only to be slammed back onto the deck by a grenade blast. A burst of gunfire stitched the length of my right leg from calf to groin. Several more rounds tore into my body.

After just a few minutes, the shooting abruptly ceased. Buddy, kneeling beside me, kept saying, "Hang in there, Mickey. We'll get you out." I was gagging and spitting up blood and trembling from the chill. I remember someone screaming into the mike for a helicopter and, later, the sound of chopper blades slapping through the predawn air. As they carried me to the chopper, I floated into darkness.

I had been hit over a dozen times by shrapnel and machine-gun bullets. Huge chunks of flesh were blown away by the .50-caliber bullets, and my right leg was shattered in two places. The top of my left hand was torn to the bone by the grenade blast.

For days I lingered near death in a field hospital's intensive-care unit. When my condition stabilized, I was evacuated to a military hospital near Tokyo, where I endured six agonizing weeks of surgery, skin grafts and traction.

My shattered left hand was held together by wire. Surgeons made a desperate attempt to salvage my leg, but it had to be amputated just above the knee.

I was sent to the Naval Hospital in Great Lakes, Illinois, for further treatment. There surgeons sewed my left hand to a stomach flap, grafting skin back onto the damaged area. I was a pathetic sight: a leg missing, an assortment of tubes running in and out of my body. And I was

weathering every conceivable type of pain, from mild aches to raw, excruciating torment. Depression was exacting its price as well.

While many around me confronted their fate with dignity and courage, others, including myself, withdrew into a sullen shell or lashed out with anger and bitter cynicism. A few of the ambulatory patients bought booze or drugs when they left the ward. We would drink ourselves into oblivion or smoke joints until we couldn't see straight—anything to relieve the pain. Most of the months I spent in the plastic- surgery ward, I was higher than a kite. That, and more than a year of taking painkillers, made me an addict.

After a year and a half, I was medically retired from the Navy. Problems persisted. Pieces of shrapnel occasionally worked their way to the surface of my body. When one particularly large chunk created a painful bump on my left arm, I called a local surgeon in Grand Rapids, Michigan, to cut it out.

A receptionist with a sweet voice answered the phone. I brazenly asked, "When are you going to take me out for lunch?" She laughed off my bold approach. When I arrived at the doctor's office, I met Shirley, the receptionist, who gave me a playful smile.

It wasn't long before we started dating regularly. We married in 1971, purchased a little house and eventually had two children.

On the surface, it looked like my life was finally going somewhere, but the changes were only superficial. A storm still raged within me, and no amount of Shirley's compassion and tenderness could calm the tempest. I was an emotional basket case, fluctuating between bitterness and fear, despair and anger.

Shirley worked steadily while I went through low-grade jobs like toilet paper. I couldn't stand meathead civilians bossing me around.

I had developed a bone disease, osteomyelitis, and suffered from recurring abscesses and infections. The pain was constant, and hardly a day passed without pain pills. I ate them like candy. For all intents and purposes, my life revolved around drugs and alcohol.

I sought healing in the VA counseling centers for Vietnam vets. They tried their best, but often we left the rap groups worse off than before. We'd pour out our grievances, only to end up stoking the flames of discontent even further.

I'd torment Shirley constantly with verbal abuse. The house was never clean enough; the food was never good enough; she never wore the right clothes.

I refused to allow her to deadbolt the door at night. I was half praying that some slob would break in so I could blow him away. I'd sit in a darkened living room with a loaded gun, drinking beer and waiting for the intruder who never came. Many nights, I never came home from work. I'd head for a bar and leave Shirley with the table set and the dinner growing cold.

Eventually both of us were empty and miserable. We decided to file for divorce.

One day Shirley and our two children were out, and the house was empty and quiet. It was 13 years since 'Nam, and everything I had touched seemed to have spoiled. I could no longer face the drugs, the infighting, our children's crying. I went to the gun cabinet and removed a .357 Magnum revolver. I walked into the bedroom, sat on the bed and stuck the barrel in my mouth. I began squeezing the trigger when I had a vision.

I saw the room as if I were floating above the bed. I saw my body sprawled on the floor, the carpet and walls splattered with blood. Then

I heard the sounds of my daughter, Jodi, and my son, Bryan, running down the hallway toward the bedroom.

I wanted to shout, "Don't look, don't look!" But they skipped into the bedroom, laughing, only to see my gory body. They burst into tears and screamed, "Daddy, Daddy!"

That's when I realized that pulling the trigger would not put an end to the suffering; it would only destroy the most beautiful gift I had. I withdrew the gun from my mouth and sank to my knees beside the bed. Tears were flowing down my cheeks—the bottled-up tears of a lifetime. For the first time in years, I prayed—an empty soul in a body racked by pain.

There were no fireworks or angelic choirs. My leg did not grow back, my scars were still unhealed, my marriage was still shattered. But a profound peace swept over me, a warm sense of knowing I wasn't alone. He understood the pain I was suffering and heard my cry. I had an almost uncanny sense that passed all understanding—like everything was going to be okay.

Shirley viewed my conversion skeptically. After years of broken promises, she had every right to distrust my assurances that I had changed. It took many months, but God helped us restore our relationship with one another and our children.

When I sit in darkness, the Lord will be a light to me.

MICAH 7

Later that year my old crewmate, Buddy Mercer, paid a surprise visit. As we sat in my kitchen reminiscing, he asked, "Do you remember that guy who bunked under you, Dave Roever, the one we called the Preacher Man?"

"How could I forget!" I said. "I never thought a guy like that would last a week."

"He didn't make it," Buddy said. "Soon after you were wounded, a phosphorous grenade blew up in his hand. He was still alive when we carried him to the chopper, but he was so badly burned, he didn't have a snowball's chance in hell."

A few weeks after Buddy's visit, Shirley called to me from another room in our house. An evangelist, a Vietnam vet, was being interviewed on a local radio show. We began listening but didn't catch the name. His conversation, however, was laced with familiar terms: SEAL Team One, PBRs. He mentioned being burned by a phosphorous grenade.

The Preacher Man? I wondered. I had to know.

After the interview I nervously dialed the radio station. When a man answered, I asked, "Is that Vietnam veteran still there?"

Anxious seconds passed; then I heard a gravelly voice. "Can I help you?"

My heart was pounding. "Were you attached to the West Coast Navy SEAL Team in the Mekong Delta in 1969?"

"Yes," he responded.

"Were you called the Preacher Man?" There was dead silence on the other end of the phone. Then, with a trace of excitement, the voice said, "Why, yes, I was."

My voice cracked. "Are you the guy who used to sleep under my bunk and tell me about Jesus?"

"Is this Mickey Block? Pervert Number One?" Half laughing, half crying, Dave added, "Man, I thought you were dead!"

For 20 minutes we laughed and cried. Finally I told him about my suicide attempt and how I had surrendered my life to God. "I'm guest minister at a church in town this evening," Dave said. "I'd love to see you and your wife."

When we arrived at the church, I was carrying an envelope. Inside was a snapshot from Vietnam and a .50-caliber slug Buddy found the night I was wounded. I handed it to one of the ushers and asked him to give the unorthodox calling card to Dave. He opened the envelope, and when the slug rolled into his palm, a large toothy grin flashed over his face.

Then Dave began to talk to the congregation. He told them about a talk show he had unexpectedly been invited to that morning, and of a phone call that catapulted him back to Vietnam. He described how the brutal realities of warfare sometimes twisted the lives of those who fought there. He spoke about one combat-hardened young man he bunked with—how he tried to reach out to him, but before he could, the youth was torn apart in a hail of bullets and grenades. He told them that he had asked God to save the man's soul before it slipped into eternity.

Many in the congregation were crying now, as if they were grieving for a lost son or brother. Then Dave said that the man had miraculously survived. His was the voice on the phone that morning, and by the grace of God he was worshiping with them that night!

Dave then asked, "Mickey, won't you and your wife stand?" Shirley and I rose amid cheers. "Mickey, please come on up." I began to limp down the aisle.

People were standing, applauding. I felt light-headed and strangely weak. I thought I would pass out. Hands reached over to steady me.

Through watery eyes I could see the Preacher Man walking toward me. His face was horribly scarred, but his eyes were filled with compassion. We met and embraced like long-lost brothers and turned to face the congregation.

There we stood, two Vietnam vets who had each taken a different fork in the road, a road that had led to the same glorious destination.

In faith there is enough light for those who
want to believe and enough shadows to
blind those who don't.

BLAISE PASCAL

NO ROOM AT THE INN

BY

DINA DONOHUE

Wallace Purling was nine that year and only in second grade. Most people in town knew that he had difficulty keeping up. He was big and clumsy, slow in movement and mind. Still, Wally was well liked by the other children in his class, though the boys had trouble hiding their irritation when Wally asked to play ball with them.

Most often they'd find a way to keep him out, but Wally would hang around anyway—just hoping. He was a helpful boy, willing and smiling, and the natural protector of the underdog. When the older boys chased the younger ones away, it was always Wally who said, "Can't they stay? They're no bother."

Wally fancied the idea of being a shepherd with a flute in the Christmas pageant that year, but the play's director assigned him a more important role. The Innkeeper did not have many lines, and Wally's size would make his refusal of lodging to Joseph more forceful.

The usual large audience gathered for the town's yearly extravaganza. Wallace Purling stood in the wings, watching with fascination.

186

Then Joseph appeared—slowly, tenderly guiding Mary—and knocked hard on the wooden door set into the painted backdrop.

"What do you want?" Wally the Innkeeper said brusquely, swinging the door open.

"We seek lodging."

"Seek it elsewhere." Wally looked straight ahead but spoke vigorously. "The inn is filled."

"Sir, we have asked everywhere in vain. We have traveled far and are weary."

"There is no room in this inn for you." Wally looked properly stern.

"Please, good Innkeeper, this is my wife, Mary. She is heavy with child. Surely you must have some small corner for her to rest."

Now, for the first time, the Innkeeper looked down at Mary. There was a long pause, long enough to make the audience tense with embarrassment.

"No! Begone!" the prompter whispered from the wings.

"No!" Wally repeated. "Begone!"

Joseph sadly placed his arm around Mary. Mary laid her head upon her husband's shoulder and the two of them started to move away. Wally stood in the doorway, watching the forlorn couple. His mouth was open, his brow creased with concern, his eyes filling unmistakably with tears.

And suddenly this Christmas pageant became different from all others.

"Don't go, Joseph," Wally called out. "Bring Mary back." Wallace Purling broke into a bright smile. "You can have *my* room."

A few people thought the pageant had been ruined. Most considered it the best Christmas pageant they had ever seen.

187

"HOLD MY HAND"

BY

RALPH KINNEY BENNETT

Aunt Inez, who had no children of her own, loved to "baby-sit" my twin brother, Roger, and me. We, in turn, loved to visit her apartment on the ground floor of the old house on Tremont Avenue in Greensburg, Pennsylvania. I remember how excited I was as Mom turned onto Tremont and the brick pavement sent vibrations through the car as we climbed the hill to "Iney's."

Roger and I would run up on her narrow, neatly swept porch and then down the cool, dark hall to the kitchen. Through the back screen door, we could see a little fish pond in the tiny yard, and beyond it, the center of Greensburg, its buildings stacked up on a hill around the gold dome of the county courthouse.

In the valley between Iney's place and the courthouse hill lay the "branch" of the Pennsylvania Railroad, where the coal, coke and passenger trains passed en route to Pittsburgh, Johnstown and Altoona. "Let's see the trains," we'd cry, and run out to the corner of Jack Street and Tremont, swinging round and round the steel street-sign pole, waiting for our aunt. She'd come out, her prematurely white hair perfectly in place, her checkered housedress crisp and smooth, her deep-set blue eyes and softly rounded cheeks catching the sunlight as she broke into a smile at our eagerness. She'd step between us and reach down. "Hold my hand," Iney would say.

We'd bolt down the Jack Street hill toward the tracks, and she'd hold us back for a moment. Her hands were soft, but the grip of her short, tapered fingers was firm and warm. We'd pull her down the hill, oblivious to how difficult it must have been for her in her high-heeled shoes. Again, she'd almost laugh the words as we tugged at her: "Hold my hand!"

At the bottom, just below the fence on a bluff overlooking the tracks, the engines rumbled by so close that we could see the engineers smiling at us as we jumped and waved, thrilling to the earthshaking roar. Sometimes there were diesels with sleek yellow stripes streaming along their black sides from the red keystone badge on their noses. But the greatest thrill was when a huge steam engine came huffing and puffing by, shooting great gouts of smoke.

Roger and I would "race the smoke," scrambling back up Jack Street with the dark cloud billowing behind us. Iney would try to keep up, holding our hands, but finally she had to let us go. We'd run ahead, shouting in mock terror at the pursuing smoke. No matter how fast we ran, the smoke always caught us, enveloping us in a cloud that stung our eyes and peppered our noses. We'd fling ourselves down laughing on the curb and wait for Iney to catch up.

Our mother and Iney, a year apart, were inseparable sisters. Iney was devoted to us—a second mother who called Roger and me "the kiddos." I remember my brother and me sitting side-by-side on the sofa watching a terrible storm pile snow outside as we waited for Iney to come out from the city for our birthday party. It was a hazardous trip through the mountains to our place in the country. The roads seemed impassable, but somehow she made it.

By countless little examples, we knew she had a firm faith and an unshakable sense of duty, tempered by a bright sense of humor. I don't believe the slightest lie ever passed her lips. She worked as a bookkeeper for a building-supply company, and her employer, Mr. Santone, once told me, "Your aunt is the most honest and trustworthy person I've ever met."

As Roger and I went off to college, got married and had children, Iney always encouraged us through sunny letters, phone calls and visits. It was on such a visit to my Maryland home, in 1984, that she suffered a stroke. It left her immobile, childlike, unable to speak intelligibly. Although she recognized us and obviously enjoyed our company, the gentle jests and easy banter were gone.

On Christmas Eve 1987, while I was outside splitting wood, I was called to the phone. Iney had been hospitalized in grave condition. I prayed for her as I walked back to the log pile. Even if I made the 250-mile drive that night, she probably wouldn't know I was there.

But as I stood in the cold, I thought of Iney alone in the hospital. I remembered her in a flowered dress, standing to applaud as I crossed the stage at my high-school graduation, and her "Well, kiddo, this is it," just before I went into the church for my wedding. I remembered that birthday party the night of the snowstorm. And I remembered a moment that had not crossed my mind for more than 40 years—a voice from long ago saying, "Hold my hand."

I drove that evening over deserted highways to the hospital. Iney awoke and smiled at me. She was worn and thin, but her eyes still had some of the old sparkle. "I know she can't talk," a nurse said to me, "but every time we check in on her she always seems to say thank you with that smile."

I sat, held her hand, prayed, and sang almost in a whisper verses from her favorite hymns. I spoke of familiar friends and happy times past. Every once in a while she gave my hand a little squeeze and smiled. I left her at 2 a.m. and drove home.

Two weeks later there was another call, and I returned to the hospital. Iney lay on her side, small and frail, her knees drawn up, her eyes staring vacantly from a face so pale it barely contrasted with her white hair. I drew a chair up to the bed, put my face close to hers and said, "Hi, Iney."

There was no flicker of recognition. "I'm sorry I'm late," I said, hoping my words were making an impression. I talked softly, read Bible verses, held her hand. When her eyes fluttered open, I looked anxiously for some sign, some spark.

I squeezed her hand tightly. It seemed lifeless. I desperately wanted to feel her fingers close on mine. I thought for a moment how human we are; how even in our most selfless moments, we still seek some small reward, some response for our efforts. Iney was oblivious to me. But I remembered her laughing eyes from long ago and her voice—"Hold my hand."

God be prais'd,
that to believing souls
Gives light in darkness,
comfort in despair!

SHAKESPEARE

Pressed between my palms, her hand remained cold, so different from that soft, warm hand that had held mine when I was young. I wept, but smiled through my tears, remembering what a happy person Iney was, remembering her pride in her "kiddos."

I realized I was squeezing her hand tightly as if I could draw her back from the brink by my own strength. I started to sing softly one of her favorite hymns, "Amazing Grace." As I sang in that darkened room I remembered how serene and sure Iney was about God's promise of life after death, how eager she had been to share that promise with others. I began to sing the last verse of the hymn. "When we've been there ten thousand years, bright shining as the sun, we've no less days to sing God's praise than when we first begun."

I felt the grip of that almost subliminal selfishness, our desire to keep a loved one with us, even as they are on the verge of life's greatest journey. I looked at her ashen face and remembered its beauty and freshness on sunny days when she, who loved to hold our hands, would finally release us so we could run happily up Jack Street.

I let go of her hand. I walked out of the room and went to sleep for a while. And when I returned, Iney's bed was empty. She was gone, and I imagined her running upward in sunlight on the happy journey that she, like each of us, must make alone.

Faith—is the Pierless Bridge

Supporting what We see

Unto the Scene that We do not—.

EMILY DICKINSON

BOTTOM DOLLAR

BY

ROBERT J. DUNCAN

Cameron Mounger and I have been friends since we were teenagers. Both of us liked music, and several years after we left high school, Cam became a disc jockey.

Recently he told me the story about the day he was down to his last dollar. It was the day his luck—and his life—changed.

The story began in the early 1970s when Cam was an announcer and disc jockey at KYAL in McKinney, Texas, and attained celebrity status. He met many country-music stars, and he enjoyed flying to Nashville in the company plane with the station owner.

One night Cam was in Nashville for the final performance of the Grand Ole Opry at Ryman Auditorium before it moved to Opryland USA. After the show an acquaintance invited him backstage with all the Opry stars. "I didn't have any paper for autographs, so I took out a dollar bill," Cam told me. "Before the night ended, I had virtually every Opry personality's autograph. I guarded that dollar bill and carried it with me always. I knew I would treasure it forever."

194

Then station KYAL was put up for sale, and many employees found themselves without a job. Cam landed part-time work at WBAP in Fort Worth, and planned to hang on to this job long enough for a full-time position to open up.

The winter of 1976-77 was extremely cold. The heater in Cam's old Volkswagen emitted only a hint of warm air; the windshield defroster didn't work at all. Life was hard, and Cam was broke. With the help of a friend who worked at a local supermarket, he occasionally intercepted dumpster-bound outdated TV dinners. "This kept my wife and me eating, but we still had no cash."

One morning as Cam left the radio station he saw a young man sitting in an old yellow Dodge in the parking lot. Cam waved to him and drove away. When he came back to work that night, he noticed the car again, parked in the same space. After a couple of days, it dawned on him that this car had not moved. The fellow in it always waved cordially to Cam as he came and went. What was the man doing sitting in his car for three days in the terrible cold and snow?

Cam discovered the answer the next morning. This time as Cam walked near the car, the man rolled down his window. "He introduced himself and said he had been in his car for days with no money or food," Cam recalled. "He had driven to Fort Worth from out of town to take a job. But he arrived three days early and couldn't go to work right away.

"Very reluctantly, he asked if he might borrow a dollar for a snack to get him by until the next day, when he would start work and get a salary advance. I didn't have a dollar to lend him; I barely had gas to get home. I explained my situation and walked to my car, wishing I could have helped him."

Then Cam remembered his Grand Ole Opry dollar. He wrestled with his conscience a minute or two, pulled out his wallet and studied

the bill one last time. Then he walked back to the man and gave him his bottom dollar. "Somebody has written all over this," the man said, but he didn't notice that the writing was dozens of autographs. He took the bill.

"That very morning when I was back home trying not to think about what I had done, things began to happen," Cam told me. "The phone rang; a recording studio wanted me to do a commercial that paid $500. It sounded like a million. I hurried to Dallas and did the spot. In the next few days more opportunities came to me out of nowhere. Good things kept coming steadily, and soon I was back on my feet."

The rest, as they say, is history. Things improved dramatically for Cam. His wife had a baby and named him Joshua. Cam opened a successful auto-body shop and built a home in the country. And it all started that morning in the parking lot, when he parted with his bottom dollar.

Cameron never saw the man in the old yellow Dodge again. Sometimes he wonders if the man was a beggar—or an angel.

It doesn't matter. What matters is that it was a test—and Cam passed.

Every breath of air and ray of light and heat, every beautiful prospect, is, as it were, the skirts of their garments, the waving of the robes of those whose faces see God.

JOHN HENRY NEWMAN

A BOY, A SNAKE AND AN ANGEL

BY

HENRY HURT

The boy and his dog shuffled through the lonesome landscape of dry brush near their isolated home in southwestern Florida. It was a mild, breezy February afternoon. Mark Durrance, 12, had finished Sunday dinner with his family and gone outside to play.

Mark was handsome, with blond hair and bright blue eyes. He felt at ease in this remote country, surrounded by vast, open land.

With him this afternoon was Bobo, a medium-sized brindled mutt with a square, friendly face. These two happy wanderers were in rough land just right for boys and dogs . . . and venomous snakes.

As Mark and Bobo were heading home, the boy spotted a bird in a cabbage palm. With his eyes fixed on the bird, he leaped over a ditch. He landed on something that seemed to roll under the pressure of his right foot. Instantly Mark felt an explosion of pain. At first it was a numbing crush like an ax being slammed down on his foot. Then a searing jolt of furious heat savaged his lower leg.

He looked down and saw the massive head of an Eastern diamondback rattlesnake plastered across his foot. Its heavily muscled maw opened across the top of Mark's shoe in a ferocious grip. The fangs had pierced the leather and become embedded just in front of the ankle-bone. Scorched with pain, the boy stared down at the snake as it seemed to gnaw slowly and deliberately on his foot.

Then Mark was aware of his dog's loud snarling and snapping at the snake. Bobo kept darting in and nipping—ten or 15 times—but the snake wouldn't let go. Then Bobo pounced and tore into the snake's head, and blood flew.

At that instant, Mark felt the serpent release its grip. He jerked his leg away, and the snake slithered off into the bushes.

Mark was 150 yards from his house. The breeze rustling through the palm leaves would obscure any cries for help. He must not panic, Mark told himself. His parents had taught him that the faster a person's blood flows, the faster a rattler's poison reaches the heart. Then Mark realized that he couldn't even move. The pain was overpowering. He felt weak all over, and everything started to get fuzzy.

Though Mark did not know it, the rattlesnake's fangs had injected a massive amount of venom directly into a vein. The poison was racing through his body, launching multiple attacks upon his respiratory system, his heart, his body's ability to clot blood. It would take a miracle for the boy to cover 150 yards over rough terrain and then mount the steps to his door.

Bobby Durrance was pruning the bushes in his front yard when his oldest son, Buddy, came screaming: "Daddy! Mark's been snake bit!" A compact, muscular man who for a dozen years has worked in the oil fields, Bobby raced for the house and found Mark on the living-room floor, unconscious, his mother, Debbie, beside him.

The boy smelled of the musky odor the Durrances had noticed when their animals had been struck by rattlesnakes. The only words Mark uttered had come calmly and peacefully from his lips as he walked

through the door: "I've been rattlesnake bit." Then he fell to the floor unconscious, violent convulsions racking his body.

Debbie tore at Mark's shoes and uncovered an ugly, purple mound that looked to be grapefruit-size on his right foot. Without a telephone, Debbie and Bobby knew they had to drive for help. They twisted a tourniquet around Mark's leg. Then, with their son in their arms, they ran to their pickup truck and took off at top speed for the health clinic 17 miles away.

"Mark was completely limp," says Debbie. "I had him cradled in my arms. I kept his nose against my face, and his breathing was getting fainter and fainter. The only thing I could do was pray." Reaching into her own childhood for words her mother had promised would always bring strength, she repeated the 23rd Psalm.

Yea, though I walk through the valley of the shadow of death, I will fear no evil: for Thou art with me.

Bobby drove fast, hogging the road, passing cars, racing for his son's life. A mile short of the clinic, the truck began to sputter. A gauge showed that the motor was overheating. Then the engine cut off completely, and the truck rolled to a stop, still in the road.

Bobby jumped out and frantically waved his arms. Drivers swerved around him. Bobby ran back to the truck and took Mark from Debbie's arms. He carried him to the middle of the road and held the boy's limp, almost breathless body up in the air like a flag.

One car slammed on its brakes. The driver, a Haitian farm worker, spoke no English, but he understood. He urged Debbie and her unconscious son into his car and followed Debbie's hand-motion directions to the clinic.

The staff there tried to stabilize the boy, but he needed more help than they could give. They started fluids, began artificial respiration and sent Mark by ambulance to the nearest hospital—ten miles away in Naples.

No man ever prayed heartily without learning something.

RALPH WALDO EMERSON

Doctor Michael Nycum, a general surgeon, was at home washing his boat when he got word of the emergency. He sped to the hospital's emergency room and was waiting as the ambulance pulled in. "By then, the boy had quit breathing on his own," says Nycum. "He was practically dead."

Over the next eight hours, four doctors and a battery of nurses worked ceaselessly over Mark. "His whole cardiovascular system was on the brink of collapse," says Doctor Nycum. "And then his kidneys shut down." The venom prevented Mark's blood from clotting—causing internal hemorrhaging. All of this was complicated by the failure of his respiratory system. "For the first 12 to 14 hours, the only thing the little guy had going for him was his heart, and that was under tremendous stress," says Doctor Nycum.

Every aspect of Mark's body was besieged by the venom, which in such quantity has a direct toxic effect on blood as well as tissues. It kills cells. The doctors gave Mark doses of antivenin, a serum derived from the blood of horses injected with snake venom. Still, medically speaking, there was no realistic chance of saving the boy's life.

"Usually, in such a drastic case, we begin to see some turnaround within a couple of hours, or we lose the battle," says Doctor Nycum. "We didn't see this with Mark. He was as critical after eight hours as he was when we first saw him."

By Monday morning, Mark had begun to stabilize. His blood pressure improved slightly. There were signs of kidney activity. But he remained in a coma.

For Debbie and Bobby the most horrifying aspect was the blood that seeped steadily from Mark's ears, mouth and eyes. And then there was the hideous swelling of every part of his body. His hands were three times normal size. He appeared to have no neck. "His eyes were swollen so tight that all we could see were the ends of eyelashes along the slits of his eyes," Debbie remembers. "And blood seeped from the slits." Before it was over, he was given 18 pints of blood.

On Tuesday, the doctors became concerned that the swelling in Mark's right leg might shut down the blood flow to his foot, forcing the amputation of his lower leg. Jagged incisions were made along his leg so the swollen tissue could expand—thus relieving the pressure on the blood vessels.

Debbie never left the hospital. She sat for hours, praying over her son and comforting him: "He may have been in a coma, but I believed he might hear my words to him and to God."

On the third day, Mark began to regain consciousness; on the fourth, he was removed from the respirator. During the first few moments, doctors listened intently as Mark spoke to his parents. Though his voice was scratchy, he told with striking clarity about how he had jumped the ditch and landed on the rattlesnake. Laughter mingled with tears when Mark said he hoped his father was not angry with him for being so careless. To the doctors, this clarity was a sign that Mark's brain had not been damaged.

Then the doctors and nurses left the bedside. Only the boy's parents remained. Debbie rubbed her son's swollen brow and gently held his bloated hand. It was during these moments, when Mark and his parents were alone in this loving cocoon of humble thanksgiving, that the boy told them of an extraordinary event that took place in the desolate field—an occurrence that harks to the Old Testament's stirring accounts of men and angels.

Mark explained with perfect composure about a white-robed figure who appeared just when he knew that he could not walk the distance to the house. The figure took him in his arms and carried him across the field and up the steps.

"I know it was God," Mark said. "He had a deep voice. I felt calm. He picked me up and carried me all the way. He told me that I was going to be sick but not to worry, that I would make it. Then He went up into the sky. The last thing I remember was opening the door to our house."

Not a particularly religious boy, Mark told his story with a serious-ness that deeply impressed his family. Knowing the valley of death through which their son had just passed, Bobby and Debbie Durrance believed every word.

As Mark improved, he and his father discussed the boy's experience. They figured that when Mark's right foot came down on the snake's midsection, the rattler whipped back and sank its fangs into his foot. While rattlers normally pull back quickly after a defensive strike, it is possible that the snake's fangs were caught in the  leather of Mark's shoe and that the chewing motion was actually the snake's effort to loosen its grip. That motion may have pumped an extraordinary amount of venom into the boy's foot. On the basis of the width of the fang marks—more than 1 1/2 inches after the swelling had subsided—and other factors, experts estimate that the snake was at least six feet in length.

As for what took place after that, it is beyond any natural explanation. What Mark says happened can never be proved, but such things never lend themselves to proof. Somehow, the boy made it 150 yards over rough terrain and up 13 steps and then opened the door to his house.

Says Doctor Nycum: "From a medical stand-point, I don't know how he could have done it." But Mark knows with absolute certainty.

Mark Durrance is a quiet boy with a direct and attentive gaze. He possesses a calmness that Doctor Nycum describes as "stoic." No single medical procedure brought him around, says Doctor Nycum, only the ceaseless energy of many people. "He's a tough little guy, and he comes from strong people," concludes Nycum. "What brought him through was a lot of hard work and a lot of praying."

Numerous skin-grafting operations await Mark, as doctors work to rebuild the tissue on his leg and foot. However, Doctor Nycum believes that Mark will suffer no lasting disability.

Mark, moreover, is eager to return to the back country with Bobo. When he grows up, he hopes to be a farmer, so he can work on the land he loves.

Mark's parents are deeply thankful for the doctors and nurses. They also wonder about the kindly Haitian farm worker. "I don't know what would have happened without that man," says Debbie. "By the time I went to thank him, he was gone. We never knew his name."

Mark understands that he goes forward in this life with a very special blessing—the sure knowledge that, as a child, he was held in the hands of God.

Giving children the means to reach inside

to pray, to start the search for solace when

there seems nowhere to turn, is like enclos-

ing a favorite blanket in their luggage.

JACQUELYN MITCHARD

THE TIMELESS WISDOM OF GENESIS

BY

BILL MOYERS

One night I woke after midnight and couldn't get back to sleep. Turning on my bedside radio, I found myself listening to a call-in show. Soon I heard a young man telling the host: "This is my birthday, and I need help to know how to live in a world that's disintegrating. I'm scared. I'm turning 18 years old in a world that makes no sense to me." His voice was pitched and filled with anxiety.

"Are you thinking of checking out?" the host blurted.

There was a long pause before the young man answered. "I don't know," he said. "All I know is, this world I'm living in is a shambles."

Other callers chimed in about how awful things are, and the young man's voice soon was lost in the chorus. But I lay there thinking about him.

My wife, Judith, and I were working on a TV series about youth violence, and my desk was piled with research about the brutalities of American life. Getting out of bed, I went to my desk and thumbed through some comic books we'd collected, with titles such as *The Warlock Five, The Avengers, The Blood Sword.* They seemed to tell youngsters that violence is their only protection in a hostile world.

Judith and I also had been trying to raise money for a new project based on Genesis, the first book of the Bible, whose stories have inspired three of the world's enduring religions— Judaism, Christianity, Islam— and the spiritual, ethical and literary imagination of Western civilization. Fund-raising for the project was difficult, however, providing evidence of the "awful taboo against intelligent, reflective discussions of religious subjects," as PBS president Ervin S. Duggan put it.

Shortly before dawn I fell asleep, still thinking of that young man's lament: *I'm turning 18 years old in a world that makes no sense to me. . . .*

A few days later I was speaking with a young television executive, who told me she belongs to a Bible study group that meets regularly. They were working their way through Genesis, trying to apply its insights to their own experience.

Among the questions they had confronted were these: Why did God create human beings in His image and allow them freedom of choice if He knew we would sin? Is sin different today? Can you trust a God who asks a father to put the knife to his son? And what about the great message of forgiveness in the story of Joseph, who was sold into slavery in Egypt by his brothers, then rose to power in Pharaoh's court and rescued from hard times the very siblings who had betrayed him? Why is forgiveness so hard for us? Is this unwillingness to forgive at the heart of our social and political predicament today?

Listening to the woman, I wished I could contact that young talk-show caller and persuade him to join this company of sojourners. In honest conversation with them, he might have found insights no talk-show host could give him.

The memory of his despairing plea spurred me to persevere with the Genesis series in the conviction that it might have something to say today to people like him.

The stories of Genesis have been familiar to me since childhood. Every Sunday evening my friends and I would participate in a Bible "sword drill" at Central Baptist Church in Marshall, Texas. Standing in a row, Bibles at our sides, we awaited the commands of our teacher—who was often, to my discomfort, my mother. There she stood, tenacious and vigilant, looking every inch the schoolmarm she always aspired to be.

"Attention!" she would bark. "Draw swords!" Up came the Bibles to rest in both hands at our waist. Then the citation: "Genesis 32:24!" Pause. "CHARGE!" Quick as a flash, we'd thumb to the appointed text, stepping forward the instant our eyes fell on it. The winner would read the verse aloud.

As our Sunday-school teachers expounded on the Bible stories again and again, they sanitized them to protect our fragile sensibilities from the less spiritual qualities of the patriarchs. Over time I formed heroic profiles in my youthful mind.

So it was not until much later that I noticed just how imperfect were the human instruments God had chosen—Abraham, quivering before Pharaoh's officials and shamelessly offering them his wife, Sarah, to save his own neck; Jacob, cowardly and cloying as he makes off with the stolen birthright; Noah, disembarking from the ark to build an altar—then drinking himself into a stupor while cursing his own grandson.

Deep in the night, wrestling as an adult with my own fantasies, disillusionments and failures, I recognize myself in these flawed characters, contending with God. Their stories retain their hold on us because they ring so true. They tell us about the struggle of real men and women to know what it means to be the people of God. This helps to explain why stories that live, as these do, assume an even fuller life when we come together to talk about them. "It is a two-way process," says Rabbi Burton Visotzky, author of *The Genesis of Ethics.* "Our insights illuminate the Bible, and Scripture illuminates our lives."

Returning to the Genesis stories for the first time in years, reading them through the lens of a lifetime of experiences, I found myself reflecting on my steps in the long progression of faith stretching back to them. Not that the stories tell me all I want to know. They are not parables offering simple lessons for life. Things don't always work out, the stories take bizarre twists, heroism is ambiguous, and I am left with questions about human nature and the nature of God.

Why was the offense of Adam and Eve so terrible as to bring about such a long fall from grace? Is the God who commissioned the sacrifice of Isaac beyond our measure of ethics? What do we make of the God so disaffected with humanity that even innocent children would perish in the mighty flood?

Genesis confronts and confounds us.

It also comforts.

My mother conducts no more Bible drills. She is 88 and frail, her memory clouded by the trauma of a fall and broken hip. On a recent Sunday I wheeled her to a worship service in the rehabilitation center, where we listened to a sermon on forgiveness. The speaker recalled the story of a Russian woman whose son was court-martialed and executed on the eve of World War II. The grieving mother searched out the soldier who had fired the single shot that killed her son, only to discover that he was critically ill and near death. She nursed him back to life—and then adopted him.

In my mind's eye I could see Joseph, opening his arms to receive his conniving brothers, weeping at their reconciliation. I looked at my mother, sitting in her wheelchair, a tear on her cheek, her eyes fixed on the speaker. For a fleeting second I imagined her 50 years ago, and I heard her say: "Attention! Draw swords! Genesis 45:14. CHARGE!"

These stories live. Their themes of forgiveness and redemption are as powerful as they were in the beginning. They tell of life in the making, of falling and starting over—of second chances. I hope that late-night radio caller, whose forlorn voice haunts me still, hears these stories. He might yet discover the restorative message of hope and purpose that the Bible affirms even in one's most desperate times, even in the midnight darkness.

Prayer is the world in tune.

HENRY VAUGHAN

"GOD'S IN MY BASKET"

BY

CHRISTOPHER DE VINCK

It's been many years since I was in high school, but one assign-ment has stayed with me always. My class was supposed to write about someone over 70, so I decided to visit a nursing home.

I went to the office, explained my assignment, and the director told me to go to room 6. The room had a bed, a chair and a picture of a rose on the wall. An elderly woman was in the chair, knitting diligently.

When I knocked, she looked up and squinted. "Yes?" she asked.

"I'm in high school," I said nervously. "I'm supposed to write an essay."

"Come in." She stopped knitting and patted the bed. "Sit here."

I sat down, and the woman returned to her knitting.

"What are you making?" I asked.

"God's in my basket," she answered.

I spoke a little louder. "What are you knitting?"

She stopped again, smiled and repeated, "God's in my basket."

I looked around the room, then peeked into her basket, just in case I might catch a glimpse of God.

"Oh, he is there," she said. "I prayed for him to come, and he has."

The woman returned to her knitting and didn't say another word. Finally I thanked her and left.

"What did you think of her?" asked the director of the nursing home.

"She says God's in her knitting basket," I said. "I think she's a little crazy."

"She was when she first arrived," the director said. "Her husband had died, and she was alone. I suggested she pray for peace, and that is what she did.

"A few months later an aide taught her how to knit. In six months she was knitting socks for everyone. At the Christmas fair she sold over $1000 worth of socks, sweaters and blankets.

"She even taught knitting in school as a volunteer. She became the most popular person in the neighborhood."

"What about now?" I asked.

"Well, now she's in her 90s and sick. But she can still knit, and she is at peace. And she says only one thing: God's in her basket."

Weeks later I received a package. Inside was a beautiful brown wool sweater just my size, along with a note from the nursing home director:

Dear Christopher,
The woman you met here asked that we send you this gift.
She thought you might like a piece of God to keep you warm.
She died three days ago. She was very happy.

THE MIRACLE OF EDDIE ROBINSON

BY

EMILY AND PER OLA D'AULAIRE

Patches of ice glistened like quicksilver in the headlights as 53-year-old Eddie Robinson guided the 42,000-pound tractor-trailer rig down Interstate 95 near Providence, Rhode Island. It was 4 a.m., February 12, 1971. On an overpass, a lone car ahead suddenly skidded broadside across the highway. Robinson cut the wheel to the right, hoping to squeeze between the sluing vehicle and the guardrail of the bridge. In the rear-view mirror, he saw his trailer start to swing out, the first stage of a dreaded jackknife.

The car recovered safely, but Robinson's cab slammed through the guardrail and came to rest in midair, dangling from the trailer pin over another highway 40 feet below. Robinson's head had whiplashed backward, punching a hole through the rear window. Drenched with blood from head gashes and soaked with diesel fuel from the dripping tanks, Robinson had only one thought—to get out fast. Opening the door, he clawed up the side of the wreck and hoisted himself to the overpass above.

At a nearby hospital, doctors stitched, x-rayed, poked, prodded, medicated—and pronounced him a very lucky fellow. Only superficial

214

wounds. By 11 a.m., he was on a bus, heading back up I-95 to his home in Falmouth, Maine, a suburb of Portland.

That night, Robinson suddenly sat up in bed, gasping with pain. Doris, his wife of 32 years, rushed him to a local doctor early the next morning. When Robinson told him he had been thoroughly examined the day before and pronounced fit, the doctor assumed his patient was only feeling his bruises. He prescribed more painkillers and sent him home to rest.

Several days later, a letter arrived from the hospital saying there was some confusion with Robinson's X rays. The doctors suspected a more serious injury and recommended that he be reexamined. The new tests revealed a concussion, fractured ribs, back sprain, and hematoma of the left hip. Robinson didn't complain—it was not in his nature. He rested and waited to get better so he could return to work.

But his health grew worse. His vision narrowed. Sometimes the world seemed to disappear before his very eyes and he thought he was blacking out. One day he stumbled into the house, visibly shaken, to announce to Doris, "I lost the whole house for a minute. I must be going blind."

Doctor Albert Moulton, Jr., a Portland ophthalmologist, found that Robinson's vision was failing rapidly and put it down to brain damage. He told Robinson that it was likely he would be permanently blind within a few months. Robinson took the news calmly. When he got home, he called the Hadley School for the Blind in Winnetka, Illinois, and arranged to take Braille and touch-typing lessons at home. By December 1971, Robinson could perceive only the difference between light and dark. His bright blue eyes had become fixed, like a doll's eyes, staring blankly ahead.

Other problems began to crop up. He lost much of the use of his right arm, and to read Braille he had to shift to his left hand. All the while he felt a circle of pressure tighten around his head, like a steel band.

Then his hearing began to go. Soon he couldn't hear Doris even when she shouted. Hearing aids helped, but it wasn't the same. He felt trapped. He'd always been active before, often working a 70-hour week; now all was darkness and quiet.

The husky truck driver kept his spirits up by focusing on his gratitude for simply being alive. No matter how bad things were, he consoled himself, there were others, somewhere, less fortunate than he.

Soon he began attending the Lutheran church across the street from his house. He forgot about feeling trapped. He rediscovered the sense of tranquillity that comes only from within.

Robinson hated to have Doris doing his jobs, so he learned to handle outside chores by feel and memory. He coiled a rope around an iron post in the middle of the lawn, tied the other end to his mower and, by going round and round as the rope unwound, was able to keep most of the grass cut. He fixed the leaky roof of his house by climbing a ladder and feeling where the shingles had crumbled.

Robinson had never had time for animals before. Now he began noticing them as he puttered quietly around the garage. Something about the blind man made the birds, chipmunks, skunks and raccoons lose their fear, for they began to approach him. Robinson clucked at them and they chattered back. He brought them food, which they ate from his hand.

On a chill January afternoon almost a year after the accident, a poultry truck overturned on a nearby highway. A young Bantam hen escaped from the wreck and made her way to Robinson's yard. When he and Doris found the fowl the next morning, her feet were frozen. They carried her to the cellar to warm her up. When Robinson heard the new creature clucking, he would cluck back—*took-took*. This became her name.

Took-Took soon became Robinson's favorite. He built her a lean-to in the yard and fashioned an elaborate series of covered passageways into the garage, where she could keep him company. Like Robinson, the chicken overcame a handicap. After her frozen feet had sloughed off, she learned to strut around on her stump-like feet as deftly as any fully toed bird.

In the winter of 1975, after shoveling the driveway, Robinson had dinner and went to bed. That night he woke up to what he calls "neon signs flashing across my chest." His symptoms indicated heart problems, and he was hospitalized for observation for close to a month. He returned home in pain; his chest and arms reacted to the slightest exertion. Even walking up the cellar steps necessitated a nitroglycerin tablet.

Yet Robinson refused to alter his daily routine—working in his garage shop, listening to his ham radio, walking into town with Doris. And, as he had every night since he lost his sight, he went into the yard and said a prayer of thanks. "I came to realize that we fail to appreciate the many wonderful things that happen around us each day. We live too fast. I slowed down to enjoy my life and was thankful."

What Eddie Robinson didn't know at the time was that he would soon have something to be truly thankful about. On June 4, 1980, at 3:30 p.m., he was tinkering in the garage when there came the roll of thunder, then sudden rain on the roof. Using his cane to guide himself around the exterior wall of the garage, he called for Took-Took. He knew he shouldn't be out in the storm, but he was worried about her. Near a poplar at the rear of the building, he stopped to listen for her answering clucks, then heard a loud snap, like a whip cracking. Lightning had hit the tree, and the charge spilled over into the ground where Robinson stood, knocking him flat.

About 20 minutes later, when Robinson regained consciousness, he stumbled to a neighbor's house and asked for a drink of water. "I think I've been hit by lightning," he said, in a daze. With knees like rubber, he returned home, drank several more glasses of water, then went to bed.

An hour later, Robinson emerged from the bedroom, still unquench-ably thirsty. He told Doris what had happened, downed a half-gallon of milk and slumped onto the sofa. Suddenly, he realized that he was see-ing the wall plaque given to him by his grandchildren. "God couldn't be everywhere," he read haltingly, "so he made grandfathers."

"What did you say?" Doris called from the kitchen. Robinson let out a yell: "I can see that sign!" Disbelieving, Doris rushed to the living room. "What time is it?" she asked, pointing to the wall clock. "Five o'clock," he answered. "Doris, *I can see!*"

Doris noticed something else. "Where are your hearing aids?" she nearly screamed in her excitement. Robinson reached for his ears, but the devices were gone. "Dear God," said Robinson. "I can hear, too!"

The 62-year-old man felt immensely tired. He ached everywhere. Worried that the lightning might have done him harm, Doris phoned a doctor's answering service. She was told to contact the emergency med-ical team, if needed, during the night, and to come in to the doctor's office in the morning. All that night Doris sat up to monitor her hus-band's breathing, still not believing what had happened.

The next day the doctor pronounced him fine. And when Doctor Moulton examined his eyes, he verified the impossible. "I can't explain it," he said. "All I know is that he definitely could not see, and now he can."

In church that Sunday, Eddie asked the minister if he could speak briefly to the congregation. Since the accident, when it was time to go to the altar, he had been led by his wife or a friend. Not this time. When the minister motioned to him, Eddie danced up the aisle—an Irish jig, he claims—to say aloud a prayer that ended, "And I have three more words to add, Lord: Thank you. Amen."

Meanwhile, the wire services picked up the story and, almost overnight, Robinson was a celebrity. Newspapers called for interviews, photographers drove to Falmouth for a picture of Robinson and his pet chicken, TV cameras arrived. ABC Television arranged for Robinson to see his grandchildren, eight-year-old Christina and nine-year-old Kimberly, for the first time on its show, "Good Morning America."

While in New York for the show, Robinson suddenly realized he no longer had to stare straight ahead. His eyes had "unlocked." Later, staying with his son and grandchildren in Virginia, he noticed that feeling was creeping back into his right arm. In fact he felt so good he mowed his son's grass. "I didn't feel a twinge of angina pain," he recalls, "and haven't had to take a pill for my heart since the lightning."

The hateful "band" around his head disappeared. And some varicose veins in his right leg have improved.

Doctors who have examined Robinson are unable to explain why his physical problems should have abated just after the lightning struck. Were his blindness and deafness indeed caused by brain damage? Or was this a psychological reaction brought on by the trauma of the trucking accident? And did that bolt from the blue set everything right again, from top to bottom? Though some may argue and puzzle over the recovery, Eddie and his family don't. "It is an act of God," says Robinson simply. "What else could it be?"

In addition to his TV appearances, Robinson has spoken to schoolchildren, telling them what it is like to be blind—as someone who has been there and back. "I've seen more in the last three months than I had in a lifetime," he says. "I now appreciate the everyday wonders of life: moonlight filtering through the leaves, the flowers in the garden, a caterpillar spinning its cocoon.

"What's more, I never gave up hope. And maybe what happened to me will give others courage to never give up." Meanwhile, his feelings about the whole ordeal are perhaps best summed up in a bumper sticker on his car: THANK GOD FOR MIRACLES.

SANTA AND THE SISTER

BY

JOSEPH P. BLANK

Only thin, white scars indicate where the three middle fingers on Julian Taubin's right hand were nearly severed. At each holiday season, Julian, a medical electronics engineer, finds himself staring at the scars, for it seems to him that he really began to save those fingers one Christmas Eve more than 30 years ago.

On that day in 1946, he was in a New York City hospital to have a nose bone deviation surgically corrected so that he could pass the medical examination for Navy flight training. Julian had been raised in a Jewish neighborhood in the Bronx, his family was Orthodox and deeply devout, and he grew up with virtually no social contact with Christmas. Christmas meant nothing to him.

Yet as he walked through the pediatrics section of the hospital early that evening of December 24, he realized what hospitalization at Christmas meant to the children there. Many were miserably lonely. Some were sobbing. He heard an adult remark, "Too bad there's no Christmas party, no Santa Claus." After returning to his bed Julian thought, "It would take so little and mean so much to help these children out of their unhappiness."

Ten years later, Julian was married, his wife, Rebecca, was pregnant with their first child, and they were living in Teaneck, a northern New Jersey suburb. Julian had never forgotten the children in the hospital that Christmas Eve when he was hospitalized, and he now proposed to the Teaneck City Club, of which he was a vice president and program chairman, that it put on a Christmas Eve celebration for the children at Holy Name Hospital in Teaneck. The suggestion caused some discussion. Was it right for a non-denominational civic group to associate such an effort with one particular faith? Julian argued that Holy Name was the only hospital in the community, that it was used by all faiths. What's more, children were children.

Finally, after nearly a year of talk, Julian's proposal was approved. In October 1958, he enthusiastically put the idea to Sister Philomena Mary, the administrator of Holy Name: "I'll be dressed as Santa Claus . . . four or five men will be Santa's helpers. There'll be gifts for all the children . . . we'll have a little band and singing." He told her that he was Jewish and that his helpers probably would be Catholics and Protestants.

Sister Philomena listened carefully, then said, "It sounds so joyful. But I will have to check with some of my people." A few weeks later, she told Julian, "If you would still like to do it, we'd love to have you." And so it was that a Catholic hospital would have a Jewish Santa Claus.

After the first meeting, Julian got the impression that the Sister, who was in her mid-60s, had forgotten his name. From then on, she simply addressed him as "Santa" or "Santa Claus." At the outset, Sister Philomena seemed to Julian somewhat formal and detached. But as they grew to know each other better, the Sister began to show a warmth of feeling that deeply touched him. He found her quietly secure, a woman of great character, and he felt a firm affection for her.

For two months, Julian and Rebecca bought and wrapped gifts. They added their own money to the Club fund—money that they ordinarily would have spent on Hanukkah gifts for each other.

At noon on December 24, 1958, five large laundry bags were packed with elegantly wrapped gifts. Julian donned his red, white-trimmed Santa costume, tied a white beard around his chin and clapped a jaunty, peaked hat on his head. He and his four helpers—a service-station owner, a minister, an architect and a musician—then drove to the hospital.

Julian was nervous. He didn't know how he would be received. Sister Philomena and several nuns awaited him at the hospital entrance. She smiled at him and said, "You're a lovely Santa Claus." Then, looking at the bulging bags, she asked, "Would you object if I asked the Lord to bless these gifts?"

"Of course not."

The celebration began with music and songs, followed by the distribution of gifts. Sister Philomena guided Julian in how to treat some of the children. "Don't mention parents to that little girl." "Don't talk about the future to that child."

The party lasted until early evening. When it was over, Julian was grateful for all the children had given him—their smiles, their laughter and appreciation. He told Sister Philomena, "I look forward to returning next year."

"You must," she said. "I will pray for you, Santa Claus."

Julian and his helpers did return to Holy Name the next Christmas Eve afternoon. During the year Julian telephoned and visited the Sister several times. The exchange of words and the brief periods of time spent together did not express their deepening friendship. Julian simply knew that each was in touch with the core of the other.

In the spring of 1960, the accident happened. It was a Saturday evening in early April, and Julian was in the basement pushing wood through a table saw for a cabinet he was making. As the wood ran through the saw he happened to look down and see spots of red paint on the floor. He figured it must have dripped from the kitchen directly above him. But how could red paint be leaking from the kitchen floor?

Although he felt no pain, Julian suddenly, sickeningly, realized what had occurred. He switched off the saw, partially closed his hand to hold the three dangling fingers, then grabbed a diaper off the basement line and wrapped it around his hand. He hurried up the stairs yelling, "Rebe, I cut my hand on the saw! Call the police! Now!"

The patrol car came within minutes. Then, with siren wailing, it sped across Teaneck to Holy Name Hospital. Julian, his diaper-wrapped hand held to his chest with his left hand, was led into the emergency room.

An intern gently opened the diaper. After several seconds, he pushed a metal can with his shoe toward Julian and said, "Drop them in the can."

Julian couldn't do it. He couldn't voluntarily throw away parts of his own body. It would change his life. Without the fingers, the new house he and Rebecca were planning could not be built. The loss would create a crisis in his career—he devised electronic systems on paper, then, using his hands, worked with technicians to build them.

He turned to a nurse and asked, "Is Sister Philomena here?"

"Yes, she's at evening prayer."

"Could you give her a message for me?"

"I can't leave the emergency room, but I'll try to get someone for you."

The nurse made a phone call, and a nun shortly appeared. "Would you please tell Sister Philomena that Santa Claus is here?" Julian asked. "I need to talk to her."

"I don't think I should disturb her."

"Please. It's important. If the Sister knew I needed her, I'm sure she would interrupt her prayers."

"I will try," the nun said.

It seemed hardly two minutes before Sister Philomena dashed in and embraced Julian. "Santa, what happened?" she asked.

Julian briefly told her about the accident, then said, "The doctor tells me to throw away the fingers. I don't know what to do. If you tell me to do it, I will."

"I will tell you no such thing," she answered. To the intern she said, "Wrap the hand exactly as it was when he came in and don't touch him." Then she hurriedly left the emergency room.

In 15 minutes, a tall, brown-haired man in a black tie and dinner jacket strode into the room. An experienced plastic surgeon, he had been reached by Sister Philomena at his home just as he was leaving for a formal dinner. After a quick examination of Julian's hand, he told a nurse to have an operating room prepared.

Julian was wheeled down a hall toward the elevators. Sister Philomena and several other sisters walked beside him, praying. In the operating room, as he slipped into the oblivion of the anesthesia, he heard the surgical sisters praying.

When Julian drifted back to consciousness, for a minute or two he had no memory of what had happened and assumed he was in his bedroom. He tried to get out of bed but was blocked by the sidebars. A man in the next bed said, "Lie down."

Then it all came back to Julian. "Are my fingers on or off?"

"I don't know."

In a half-hour, the surgeon and Rebecca entered the room. "They're on," the surgeon told him. "We'll have to wait to see what happens."

Do not pray for easy lives.

Pray to be stronger men.

JOHN F. KENNEDY

For a time after his release from the hospital the fingers were in doubt. Numbness persisted. The nails fell off. He had to return twice for additional surgery. But gradually the three fingers grew in strength, sensitivity and mobility.

Julian felt that his hand had been reborn and he told Sister Philomena that he owed his wholeness to her. If she had not been there when he needed her, the fingers would have been lost. The Sister protested that it was not her doing; it was the way God worked.

That Christmas, Santa Claus returned to the hospital. His right hand was swathed in bandages from a skin-graft operation. When the children asked about it, Julian made light of "a little accident." It would have been difficult for him to explain that the bandages really were beautiful Christmas wrappings around the most marvelous of gifts.

Faith is like radar that sees through the fog—

the reality of things at a distance that the

human eye cannot see.

CORRIE TEN BOOM

MY INVESTMENT
IN SPRING

BY

PATRICIA SULLIVAN

I had promised myself I really *would* get up early. But as I groped for my shrilling alarm clock, rising at dawn to prepare a garden for planting seemed futile. *Why bother,* I reasoned, *when all the children are grown and gone?*

Ever since our last son and his bride moved from our Wisconsin farm to work in the city, I was alone most of the time. My husband, Chuck, worked in the city too. Lonely, I began sleeping late five days a week and seemed to come to life only on weekends.

When I finally dragged myself out of bed, I remembered that the fence line had to be checked to make sure the horses were safely penned. When I came to the old farmhouse that stood empty just inside our property, I noticed a window was broken and the front door stood ajar. The bicycles my son had left behind were missing. I reported the theft to the sheriff.

The following week, he called to say they'd caught the thieves. Would I come down to sign a complaint against them?

"You bet I will!" I said angrily. "Did you get the bikes back?"

"Well, Pat, we have one bike here, but somebody stole the other from the culprits. I guess you could call that poetic justice."

When I arrived, I asked the sheriff, "Where are the thieves?"

"Sitting in the hall," he replied.

The only people there were two skinny boys with unkempt hair and big, fearful eyes. They reminded me of two skittery chipmunks.

"Sheriff, are you sure you—?"

"They're the guilty ones, all right," he snorted. "They've admitted everything."

Then Judge Bennett swept into the room in her robes, and the sheriff went to fetch the boys. They came in with heads hanging.

"Wait a minute," I said. "Can't we work this out?" My mind was racing. *Work—that could be the answer.* "Judge Bennett, why can't the boys work for me this spring?" I asked. "They could earn enough to pay for the missing bike. I could use a little help, and the boys will learn the value of a dollar."

Judge Bennett peered at me over her eyeglasses and replied, "Well, I hope you know what you'll be getting into. But all right." A juvenile officer would check on the boys once a week.

The following Saturday at exactly 7 a.m., I awoke to a knock on the back door. The boys were standing on the porch, shivering in the early-morning chill.

"Come inside," I invited. "You didn't have to be here so early. Nine would have been okay. How about breakfast before we start?"

In a few minutes we were sitting down to scrambled eggs, sausages and pancakes. The boys seized their forks.

"Whoa, not so fast, fellas. Around here we say grace first."

While I said the prayer, they rolled their eyes and glanced slyly at each other. As they ate, they told me they were ten and 11 years old, but both were in the same class at school. The 11-year-old had moved three times in the past year since his parents' divorce. The other boy's mother

had been depressed for several months following the death of her husband.

We worked in the garden until we heard the noon whistle. Because I was so tired, we ended up at the local drive-in for hamburgers. I asked the boys to be at work at nine o'clock Monday, the start of their spring vacation.

The next morning I was again awakened at seven. *Oh, no, not on Sunday too!* Sure enough, it was the boys I'd come to call Chip and Dale.

"We have a present for you," said Chip as Dale thrust a garter snake at me.

I gritted my teeth and handed it back. "Thank you very much, boys. "Now please put it in the garden where it can do some good eating insects."

The boys looked at each other as if to say, "What kind of a woman is this, to thank us for a snake?"

Monday came too soon. I had to show the boys the difference between vegetable seedlings and weeds. They had a thousand questions, and we got into an hour-long discussion on ecology, wildlife and rock bands. After they put away a huge lunch, I read them a story I had written to amuse my children years before.

On the dot of seven the next morning came the familiar knock.

Dale said, "We really have a lovely present for you today, Mrs. Sullivan," as Chip handed me the biggest, fattest blacksnake I had ever seen.

This has gone far enough, I thought. "Look out, boys, this is a Coluber constrictor!" I yelled and tossed it back at them. They dropped it and ran.

When they finally came back, I said, "Now, boys, I want you to know something about me. I raised nine children, and there is no trick that hasn't been played on me before. If you can't come up with something better than some old snakes, don't even bother to try to scare me anymore."

They gave me a respectful look.

The boys shoveled and raked. They dug and divided peonies and irises. They watered and weeded and helped pick the produce from the seeds they had planted. We worked together all summer, and I began rewarding them with hikes and picnics. In early fall we planted tulip bulbs, daffodils and crocuses. When the boys asked why I bought so many "old dead bulbs," I told them they would turn into beautiful flowers—they were my "investment in spring."

All summer I had been baking treats I hadn't made in years. Together we made gingerbread men, pies and cookies.

"Those boys are walking stomachs," I told my husband.

"This boy too," Chuck said. "We haven't eaten this well in a long time."

Each week I reported "no problems" to the juvenile officer.

The boys paid off their debt and even earned enough to buy bikes of their own. They went to school, but still came back to help on Saturdays and holidays. They proudly showed me their improved report cards.

One Saturday I missed the familiar seven-o'clock knock. "I wonder where the boys are," I said to Chuck.

"Don't worry about those guys," he replied, laughing. "They can take care of themselves."

"Yes," I said, "but I think they changed for the better, don't you?"

Chuck laughed again. "They're not the only ones who changed for the better. You haven't been this content since we had the whole brood at home. I guess it's true what they say—that whatever you sow, so shall you reap."

Then came the familiar knock, and I fairly leaped to answer it.

The following spring, when I came home from ten days in the hospital, Chip and Dale rode their bikes all the way from town to visit me—as usual, at 7 a.m. They presented me with a big bouquet of the tulips we had planted.

We went into the kitchen, and I set out the raspberry jam we'd made, along with some biscuits and milk. As I picked up a biscuit to take a bite, both boys said in unison, "Whoa, not so fast! Around here we say grace before we eat!"

I looked up sheepishly to see them beaming at me. My investment in spring had just bloomed.

All the scholastic scaffolding falls, as a
ruined edifice, before a single word: faith.

NAPOLEON BONAPARTE

OUR MYSTERIOUS PASSENGER

BY
IRA SPECTOR

*T*he midday sun beat down on my wife, Barbara, and me as we walked across the tarmac to the terminal at Loreto International Airport on Mexico's Baja peninsula. We were flying our single-engine plane home to Calexico, California, later that day, ending a week's vacation.

A tall man stood near the terminal, nervously dabbing at his face and neck with a handkerchief. I had noticed him earlier, watching us as we readied our plane.

Suddenly he approached, blocking the doorway. He was in his 40s and looked as if he had spent the night in the terminal. "Excuse me," he said, removing his Panama hat. "Can you help me out? I'm an American and I got bumped from the flight to Los Angeles. I need to catch my connecting flight to Florida."

Trying to muster an authoritative tone I said: "I'm sorry, but I've already filed my flight plan with the airport commandant. It only allows me to take my wife out of the country. Why don't you get a later flight?"

"There isn't another flight until tomorrow, and I've got to leave today," he insisted.

234

"Well, we're only going to Calexico, at the border."

"That's okay," the stranger said. "Let's go to the commandant's office and ask if I can leave with you." He turned to enter the building.

"Wait a minute," I said uneasily. "I don't have an oxygen mask for you, and we're flying at 14,500 feet. You'd feel altitude sickness."

"That's okay. I'm in good shape."

"And there's no room for additional luggage," I added, glancing at his suitcase. "The plane's full."

"I'll hold the bag on my lap."

At this point Barbara asked, "Would you excuse us for a second? I need to talk to my husband."

"Sure." The stranger stood aside to let us enter the terminal.

Barbara, a trial lawyer and the voice of reason in the family, whispered, "Are you crazy? You want to risk our lives by giving a ride to some strange person who could be a fugitive or a terrorist?" Her voice was rising. "What if he hijacks us?"

"Something tells me he's legitimate," I said. "Maybe it's payback time." I was thinking of when Barbara and I had flown to Mexico ten years earlier. We had ridden a little motorcycle into the desert and lost our way. We were sweaty, sunburned and covered with dust when we finally made it into a town. We met some American pilots and asked if they could take us to our plane, but they walked away. Finally some California college students got us back to our plane.

"Remember being stranded down here years ago?" I asked. "Let's go to the commandant's office and see what he says. I doubt he'll allow him to go with us, but I'd feel better if we at least asked."

The commandant listened to the stranger's story, glanced at his tickets and quickly changed our passenger number from a "1" to a "2." The entire transaction took about a minute.

Now I had to take the stranger with us. Not knowing what else to do, I wandered off in the direction of our plane. Barbara walked beside me, glaring straight ahead. To break the tension, I turned to the stranger following us and asked his name. "Virgil," he said.

Cruising northwesterly at 14,500 feet, Barbara and I sat in silence, breathing oxygen from our masks. I looked back at Virgil, seated behind her. Strangely, the lack of supplemental oxygen didn't seem to bother him. He nodded back at me and smiled. I was beginning to think things might work out. The drone of the engine had a soothing effect, and an unusually strong tail wind promised to put us in Calexico well ahead of schedule. Virgil's chances of making it to Los Angeles were improving by the minute. Yes, maybe things would work out after all.

Not everyone felt the same way, though. Barbara had her arms folded across her chest and her head hunched down as if she expected a hatchet blow from behind.

Just north of the border, I became more concerned with the weather than with Virgil. The ride grew turbulent, with wind gusts causing our plane, a Mooney 231, to rattle.

Suddenly we plunged 100 feet in a downdraft. Barbara glanced nervously at me. The radio warned of strong, gusting winds with blowing dust and sand throughout California's Imperial Valley. Visual flight was not recommended.

Looking toward Calexico, I could see a strange, dark-brown cloud spanning the horizon. A sandstorm! In my 23 years of flying, I had never witnessed anything like it.

Calexico is a small field unequipped for instrument approaches. If we couldn't land visually, our depleted fuel and the increasingly turbulent ride would mean flying back to Mexicali on the Mexican side of the border. I shivered as I imagined the air filter clogging up and the engine quitting.

Even if we made it, our unexpected arrival at Mexicali would surely get the attention of some savvy border official. We could be held up for days while our passenger, whom we knew nothing about, was being investigated. Virgil wasn't the only one who had to get back to work.

Whack! Turbulent air jolted me out of my musings, causing the plane to pitch up. *Whap!* Now the nose pitched down, spilling my maps on the floor. I decided that we were going to Mexicali, and probably to jail.

Just as I retrieved the maps from the floor, Barbara exclaimed, "I see Calexico!"

There it was, only five miles in front of us. The sand-storm was swirling all around the airport, but the runway was in the clear.

I banked the plane toward the runway, praying that the hole over the airport would remain open a bit longer. As I eased into our final turn, we encountered wind shear, setting off a wail from the stall-warning alarm. I jockeyed the throttle back and forth. Barbara was fright-ened, yet her look told me, *You can do it.*

Suddenly the air smoothed out, and we were down. As we turned off the runway, the sandstorm closed in around us. In all my years of flying, this was my closest call.

I looked back at Virgil—and I couldn't believe how calm he was. He was sitting there reading, and of all things, he was reading a Bible. He smiled as he put it away.

Inside Calexico's airport, Barbara sipped coffee and looked out at the sand blowing across the landscape. Finally she said, "Well, what do you make of him?" I still wasn't sure.

Just then, Virgil came to the table. I asked him about his prospects for getting to Los Angeles. People weren't even driving in this weather.

"I found a commuter flight leaving from Imperial Valley Airport, a few miles from here. Unfortunately, they don't know when it will take off. On top of that, the flight is sold out. But just in case, I called a cab. Maybe someone will cancel."

I knew the time had come to learn more about this stranger. "What were you doing in Loreto?" I asked.

Virgil stared into his coffee cup. "My wife and I were in a terrible accident in Loreto ten years ago. We were with another couple on vacation, touring Baja in a rented motor home. The other couple was in the front, and we were in the back. Suddenly the right tire went off the road, and we rolled down an embankment. We were carrying 160 gallons of fuel. The butane tank for the stove exploded. There was a horrible fire. I managed to escape out the back window, and my wife squeezed through the door.

"The other couple was trapped inside, screaming for help. I tried to pull them out through the front window, but I couldn't. It was too late.

"My wife and I were burned pretty badly," he continued, "and my spleen had ruptured. We were several miles from Loreto. We crawled up the embankment and tried to flag down someone to help us. Finally a Mexican fellow pulled over and rushed us to the Health Center of Loreto.

"They saved our lives. But the clinic was poorly equipped. The operating table looked like an old ironing board. I spent the night in a dental chair—there was no bed.

"We were transferred to a burn unit in California. But I vowed that I would come back and give the clinic money to buy proper equipment and medical supplies."

"And your wife?" I asked.

238

"She had skin grafts, and she's doing fine. I guess I buried the whole experience in the back of my mind. I'm starting my own business—a boat-sales company. I hadn't thought about the accident until last Saturday."

Virgil took a deep breath. "I awoke with a start. Something told me I needed to act on that vow I made ten years ago. I arrived in Loreto yesterday. The health center was still in bad shape—the paint was peeling, the bedsheets were torn, and broken windows were covered with tinfoil. I wrote them a check. It wasn't a large sum, but they were extremely grateful. You should have seen the looks on their faces."

"I'll bet," I said.

"This morning, the flight to Los Angeles was full, and I was left stranded. Then I saw you folks."

We sat in silence a moment. Then a man approached our table—it was the cabdriver Virgil had called. Virgil hurriedly picked up his hat and bag. "Thanks again, folks," he said.

"Wait, Virgil." I handed him a business card. "Let us know if you make it aboard that flight."

I returned home and settled into my routine, still thinking about Virgil and the lesson he had taught me: we were aided by strangers when we were stranded many years before, so we helped Virgil. After the accident, Virgil and his wife were helped by the people of Loreto, so he returned to help them. These were links in a growing chain of kindness, and each kindness we do, I now recognize, always comes back to us, sometimes in mysterious ways.

One day, we received a letter from Virgil, written on the letterhead of his boat-sales company: "Just a short note to say thanks once again. I made my flight out of Imperial Valley. The plane was loading as I arrived at the gate. I got the last seat. Love, Virgil."

MESSAGE OF THE
WHITE DOVE

BY

DEWEY ROUSSEL

From his first day at school, our son Hubert—we called him Bubs—had shown a keen and protective interest in birds. "St. Francis of Assisi Preaching to the Birds" was one of the pictures in his room. He joined the National Audubon Society, read the literature and lore of ornithology, and trapped wild birds to band them for study, then set them free.

In spring and summer, Bubs would lie under the trees watching, through the lacing of leaves, the silent and majestic poetry of vast cumulus ranges shaping and merging and reshaping themselves in a drama of color and movement. He spent hours admiring the birds' effortless flights, amused by their comic or petulant antics.

As Bubs grew older, he was drawn to flying. Pictures of aircraft went up next to the one of St. Francis. He became fascinated with what men had learned from the anatomy and habits of birdlife in the evolution of mechanical flight.

He was 17 on that gloomy Sunday afternoon when Pearl Harbor was bombed. Bubs greeted his father and me with the shocking news. I do not remember his words; I remember only the look in his eyes.

When the Army call came, he let us know that, somehow, he would serve in the air.

The Army put him in a clerical job, but he volunteered for flight training. Schooled for a tedious year as a radio operator on the newly developed B-29s, then undergoing secret tests, Bubs finally arrived at a Kansas air base, where his dream was realized.

During the months that followed, his letters reflected an almost mystic exhilaration. "It seems so pure and clean in the air," he wrote. "Like giant birds, we glide, circling above the clouds, completely free and detached from the confusion and detail of earth."

When his letters were interrupted, we understood. It was December 1944. The war had reached what everyone felt must be its decisive phase. In Europe, the Allies were threatening Germany; in the Pacific, the bombing of Japan had revealed that the B-29s were making runs from the Mariana Islands.

His next letter let us know that his base was Saipan—a tiny island in the western Pacific. It was in that distant, strange and desolate theater of terror that boys turned into men. Bubs was the youngest in his crew.

Exactly how, when or where Bubs's plane went down is still a mystery. The official report gave only the usual meager details: four of the planes that soared out over the Pacific in the early morning of December 13, 1944, to make a bomb run on factories at Nagoya, were never heard from again.

Families of the crewmen of "our" plane clung desperately to hope. We wrote encouraging letters to one another. But we were the only family to receive a letter from the missing after the loss. Bubs had placed it on his pillow:

> *Dear Folks: I have left this with instructions to send it on to you if anything happens to me. I send you my love and blessings. My life has been a full one. I have been loved like very few persons ever. I love you all with the best*

*that is in me. It hasn't been hard for me, knowing you believe in me, trust me
and stand behind me in fair or foul. Knowing this has made me strong. . . .*

I typed copies for the relatives of the other lost crewmen. Bubs's letter brought us close together in the bonds of a mutual sorrow.

On the first warm spring day following the war's end, we had a family reunion. In the late afternoon, we moved out onto the lawn. The yard was lush with new grass; the pear trees were white with blossoms. From

the hummingbirds in the honeysuckle vines to the sparrows in the hedges, the yard was alive with the sights and sounds of the earth being reborn.

As we sat talking, suddenly three lovely white doves swooped down around us, then whirled away over our heads. We were startled.

After a few minutes, my brother, who had just returned from two years' service in Europe, rose to leave. I followed him through the house, out onto the front lawn. As he turned to wave good-bye, he pointed to the house-top.

"There they are, Dee," he remarked. "That looks like sights you see in Europe. Where did they come from?"

I looked up. There, on the peak of our roof, were the three white doves, perfectly still against the blue sky.

I answered that I had never seen them before.

My brother drove away. As I walked back into the house, the phone rang. It was a friend, the wife of one of the crew members.

"I still have hope for the boys," she said.

"I know how you feel," I replied. "But why should we feel hopeful? Certainly we have received no encouragement from the government."

"But I do feel we will hear from them," she insisted.

"Why?" I pressed.

"Because I have prayed so hard," she said. "I asked God to send me a sign that they are safe. And . . . He *has!* He sent a white dove to our house!"

I could not speak. I merely asked her to visit the next day.

That night I found it hard to sleep. I could think only of the doves that had come to our house and to my friend's house. Was it all a coincidence?

I rose early the next morning and, trembling, stepped into the yard. But when I turned and looked up, my heart fell. The doves were gone.

Quickly I picked up and opened the paper and glanced at the headlines, seeing nothing, merely trying to hide my disappointment.

But I continued walking toward the garden. As I rounded the corner of the house, my eyes lifted to the peak of our garage. There, facing me, his feathers radiant in the glow of the rising sun, was a beautiful white dove!

In that moment, a wonderful calm filled my heart. It abides with me still. I know I will never see Bubs again in this life. But I understand, too, that all is well with him.

ACKNOWLEDGMENTS

All the stories in *Doorways of Faith* previously appeared in *Reader's Digest* magazine. We would like to thank the following contributors and publishers for permission to reprint material:

My Angel in Disguise by James Dodson. © 1994 by James Dodson. Yankee (December '94).

Child Choking! by Les Brown with Annamae Cheney. "The Earthmover" by Les Brown & Annamae Cheney. Reprinted with permission from **Guideposts** magazine. Copyright © 1979 by Guideposts, Carmel, New York 10512.

Little Dog Lost by Donna Chaney. "A Long, Long Way" by Donna Chaney. Reprinted with permission from **Guideposts** magazine. Copyright © 1983 by Guideposts, Carmel, New York 10512.

Chain of Life by Philip Zaleski. ©1989 by Parenting Magazine Partners. Parenting (December '89/January '90).

"I Have Not Forgotten" by Hilary Leidolf Lohrman. Reprinted with permission from **Guideposts** magazine. Copyright © 1995 by Guideposts, Carmel, New York 10512.

Every Evening by Joanne Kaufman. © 1997 by Time Publishing Ventures. Parenting (December '97/January '98).

Because of Adam by Henri J. M. Nouwen. © 1988 by Henri J. M. Nouwen. Weavings (March/April '88).

Me and the Preacher Man by Mickey Block with William Kimball. "BEFORE THE DAWN" by Mickey Block with William Kimball, copyright © 1988 by Mickey Block. Published by Daring Books.

No Room at the Inn by Dina Donohue. Reprinted with permission from **Guideposts** magazine. Copyright © 1966 by Guideposts, Carmel, New York 10512.

Bottom Dollar by Robert J. Duncan. © 1993 by Robert J. Duncan. McKinney Living (Fall '93).

The Timeless Wisdom of Genesis by Bill Moyers. "GENESIS" by Bill Moyers, copyright © 1996 by Public Affairs Television. Used by permission of Doubleday, a division of Random House, Inc.

God's in My Basket by Christopher de Vinck. "SIMPLE WONDERS" by Christopher de Vinck, copyright © 1995 by Christopher de Vinck. Published by Zondervan Publishing House.

My Investment in Spring by Patricia Sullivan. Reprinted with permission from **Guideposts** magazine. Copyright © 1985 by Guideposts, Carmel, New York 10512.

Quotations

Reverend Charles L. Allen (permission granted by the author); *Jacquelyn Mitchard* in Parenting (December '99/January '00); *Corrie Ten Boom*, "TRAMP FOR THE LORD" (Revell). Biblical scriptures are from the "REVISED STANDARD VERSION OF THE BIBLE," National Council of the Churches of Christ in the USA (Thomas Nelson).

The quotation by Abbe Huvelin was originally published in the English Church Review (1911).

Photo Credits

Cover: MaryEllen McGrath/Bruce Coleman; title page: Rosanne Olson/Graphistock; pp. 2-3: Zephyr Images; p. 5: James Marshall/Corbis; p. 7: Kamil Vojnar/Photonica; pp. 8-11: Photodisc; pp. 12-13: Art Resource; p. 15: Michael Gesinger/Photonica; p. 18: Art Resource; p. 21: Zefa Zeitgeist/Photonica; pp. 22-23: James Balog/Stone; p. 25: H. Reinhard/Bruce Coleman; p. 27: Kamil Vojnar/Photonica; pp. 28-33: Photodisc; pp. 36-37: B. W. Hoffman/Envision; pp. 39-45: Photodisc; p. 47: Sandford Agliola/Stock Market; p. 51: Kenro Izu/Graphistock; pp. 52-53: Photodisc; p. 55: David Wells/Photonica; pp. 58-59: Photodisc; p. 60: Jana Leon/Graphistock; pp. 62-64: Photodisc; pp. 66-67: Gary Withey/Bruce Coleman; p. 69: Photodisc; pp. 70-71: Ken Whitmore/Stone; pp. 73-77: Photodisc; pp. 78-79: B. W. Hoffman/Envision; p. 80: Photodisc; p. 82: Gary Withey/Bruce Coleman; pp. 84-85: Photodisc; p. 88: Joanne Dugan/Graphistock; pp. 90-94: Photodisc; p. 99: Penny Gentieu/Stone; pp. 100-105: Photodisc; p. 108: Jake Wyman/Stone; pp. 112-113: Rob Lewine/Stock Market; p. 114: Photodisc; p. 115: Jennifer Baumann/Graphistock; pp. 116-149: Courtesy Father William J. Witt and Robert A. Calcagni; pp. 150-151: Library of Congress/American Heritage;